A MEASURED RESPONSE: THE UNITED GLOBAL SECURITY PARTNERSHIP

PETER MACRAE

Additional Publications

The Poppies of Mohammed

Al Qaeda, the Taliban and Afghan heroin - A fact-based novel

Twenty-First Century Violent Conflict: The Insufficiency of International Law

Website

Peter MacRae A Measured Response

A MEASURED RESPONSE: THE UNITED GLOBAL SECURITY PARTNERSHIP

Peter MacRae

SECOND EDITION

May, 2015

ISBN: 1514278839
ISBN 13: 9781514278833

As with the First Edition,
This book is dedicated to my wife
Patricia.
Her enthusiasm for my efforts, her review,
ideas and patience
are greatly appreciated.
I probably would not have written this book
without her support.

A MEASURED RESPONSE:
THE UNITED GLOBAL SECURITY PARTNERSHIP
Is also dedicated to a dear friend,
John Quigley.
John passed away during the writing of the First Edition.
He never read it, nor for that matter,
did he even know I was writing it.
That is probably just as well.
As with every other subject, we would have argued endlessly.
I have missed him.

TABLE OF CONTENTS

PREFACE

In a moment of grief, frustration and anger I sent a "Letter to the Editor" to the San Diego Union Tribune, The Los Angeles Times, The New York Times and The Washington Post on September 11, 2001. It was the evening of the most devastating attack on American soil, with the greatest loss of life since the American Civil War. Using four hijacked commercial airliners, killing all aboard in the subsequent suicide crashes, terrorists destroyed the World Trade Center and surrounding office buildings in New York City and damaged the Pentagon in Washington, D. C. On the fourth airliner passengers fought the highjackers, bringing the airplane down in a Pennsylvania field. Fortunately, to my knowledge, none of those papers published the letter:

> *"Dear Editor:*
>
> *Years ago, when the Soviet Union was the second most powerful nation on earth, some of my friends laughed at me when I made the following suggestion. I proposed that the U.S. and the USSR come to a unique agreement for stability in the Middle East. At the same moment in time high ranking U. S. and Soviet diplomats pay a visit to the top leaders of all the states in the Middle East. Their message, "You have 24 hours to steal as much money from your treasury as you wish, dismiss your military (allowing senior officers to participate in the theft) and leave, because in 24 hours we will own this land! At which point, we and the Soviet Union divide the administration for the region.*
>
> *In light of the events of September 11, 2001, my view has changed slightly. Because of the demise of the Soviet Union and the weakened*

state of the Russian Federation, I would invite Russia, Great Britain and Germany to such a partnership.

If one thinks it is not a feasible plan, look at the greed factor. While, as a public relations gesture, the Russians might do some posturing, the sure prospect of a large share of Middle East oil and the need for Western financial support would allow them to see the wisdom of such a plan. As for the Middle Eastern leaders, if they are convinced they will die, their egos will probably convince them that a life of luxury on a sunny coast is not a bad idea.

To those states who would doubt the resolve, the action on our united part should be swift, massive and decisive. At the point of control, we should impose a settlement upon Israel and the Palestinians. During the settlement process, under the partnership martial law, we should, with swift action that leaves no mistaken impressions, tolerate no violence.

We should have no concern whatsoever for world opinion. Too many people have been killed or injured, too many lives have been irreparably damaged. It is time, while the consequences of such an action may be severe, to end this worldwide problem. History, in just the last century, is full of far greater tragedies because of the careful diplomatic and soft military handling of zealots.

Peter Heinig*
Campo, California"

A somewhat naive and emotional position, yes. It was written at a time when we still did not know the full extent of the number of lives, innocent lives, lost. Nor, for that matter, did we know the economic losses suffered by the United States and the Free World. We did not know, at that writing, who the enemy was that committed this "act of war". We did, however, have strong suspicions. Communication intercepts almost immediately pointed to al Qaeda.

My emotions have long since subsided. In fact, upon reflection, I was going to leave this "Letter to the Editor" out of the preface to this work. I decided to leave it. It is demonstrative of the kinds of emotions that, while not carefully considered, are shared by many angered and frustrated people. At times of international crisis we have all heard emotional comments such as, "We ought to blast them back to the stone age.", or, "We ought to nuke em.". Besides not being very practical solutions, basic underlying problems are not solved and new ones are created.

Throughout history violence has not achieved world peace and stability. Nor has diplomacy achieved world peace. It has been very difficult to get the diplomats to agree, and their actions or inactions are seen as weakness in some quarters. Sanctions against states have not enjoyed great success either. Therefore, if none of these approaches have been successful in achieving man's elusive dream of lasting world peace and security, what do we do?

Though only one layman's ideas, what you are about to read is a reasoned and thoughtful work on eliminating terrorist and other "rogue" violence in the world. The principles which will be advocated in this work could be effective in controlling other problems facing civilized man. In addition to the controlling of terrorism and world security we will devote a chapter specifically talking about the war on drugs.

Very few of the ideas and principles set down in this work are original. However, the purpose of this work is to bring together principles that have been known but, unfortunately, have not been followed on a worldwide scale. It is the purpose of this work to establish that a well-disciplined, permanent organization must enforce world security, and no state can do that alone.

This work will necessarily focus on the Middle East and Southwest Asia but not forgetting the African continent. That is necessary because these areas are the current theatres and staging grounds for much of the uncontrolled violence in today's world. However, I believe that if the ideas put forth in this work were followed they would work in any part of the world, at any time.

Throughout this writing, "nations or nation/states" will be referred as "states", because "states" is the more proper term.

John Locke, the seventeenth century British philosopher, said that, "man forms government to protect himself from himself".(1) From early on man recognized the need for power, possession and control. In some cases, this has been the uncontrolled excessive need. At the basic level, tribes were formed with a chieftain and possibly a council to make and enforce the rules of their society and maintain order. Some societies are still run by this system. Later, city states and finally, nation/states, fulfilled the same role on a larger scale.

While most members of society are socialized (civilized) and peaceful, there always have been and always will be "rogues" who will exploit weaknesses where they find them to satisfy their unreasonable needs. Were the last statement not true, there would be no need for locks, police forces or militaries. Because these individuals or groups have always and will always exist, creating conflict, the idea of ultimate world peace is a "pipe dream" unless a system is put into place to enforce peace.

This work will look at history. It will examine the nature of the threat to world peace and security in the first half of the twenty-first century. A plan will be created for the formation of an international organization named THE UNITED GLOBAL SECURITY PARTNERSHIP (UGSP). The justification and the precedence for the plan will be detailed. The plan, its partners and its execution will be clear. There will be an outline of the decision-making criteria the UGSP should use to take action to enforce world security, and we will describe those actions. There will also be a discussion of the administration of those states, which if necessary, must be occupied. The work will deal with the return of those states to self-rule.

The roles of the United Nations and the International Criminal Court, acting with the UGSP will be explained. There will be a discussion of how an entity such as the UGSP could be funded. The work will examine how peaceful solutions to world-threatening problems can be achieved with the help of, or the threat from the UGSP.

With the UGSP as the "world's policeman" there will be a discussion of how the economic conflict between "guns or butter" can be moved in the favor of "butter". It will be clear as to why it is in the economic interest of many states to make peace with the rest of the world and how, if they fail to do so, they could fail as states.

It is envisioned that the UGSP would investigate and analyze each world threatening situation objectively, not emotionally or politically. This requires *A MEASURED RESPONSE*, a step by step plan developed to cure the problem. The offending entity and the world will be clearly informed of that measured step by step plan with the clear understanding of the certainty of its execution. With respect to that plan, the measured response will be the transition from one step or phase to the next severe phase of the plan if the offending entity does not acquiesce to the order of the UGSP. The work will show how a non-emotional, non-political measured response and the plan of the UGSP, executed absolutely, could lead to world peace and stability.

Throughout this work it will be stressed that no one state, no matter how powerful, can police world security alone. No one state can, nor should, sustain the economic burden. The responsibility and the burden must be shared.

In the realm of international relations, political scientists love to study and argue a myriad of theories as to how states behave politically and how they interact. In this author's view there are two theories which are truly important. *Idealism* is the first. Simply stated, Idealism posits "how things ought to be". *Realism* is the second. Over simplified, Realism says that states will always act in their own best interest. It is "how things really are".

The ideas and proposals set down in this work clearly fall in the realm of Idealism. This author believes there is little chance that the community of states will ever enact such a plan. Why? Because all international agreements are voluntary, and it is doubtful that any state would want to subject itself to such an organization. In large part, it is a problem of sovereignty. Nonetheless, these ideas need to be in their thinking and just maybe, considered.

Two final notes: This revised edition has been written in 2015. The original publication of *A MEASURED RESPONSE: THE UNITED GLOBAL SECURITY PARTNERSHIP* was written in 2001(2); *My surname was Heinig before doing a legal name change in 2003, to my family's ancestral Scottish name, MacRae,

A SUMMARY OF THE PLAN

THE UNITED GLOBAL SECURITY

PARTNERSHIP

The United Global Security Partnership (UGSP) will be a global police force made up of states committed to controlling terrorism and other threats to world peace and security. It will become involved with conflicts within an individual state's boundaries where there exists genocide or gross violations of human rights as defined by International Law. The UGSP will become involved where conflict spreads beyond a single state's borders or there is a credible probability that it will. It will not be a temporary organization such as the "Desert Storm" coalition against Iraq in 1991. Rather, it will be a permanent partnership such as the North Atlantic Treaty Organization (NATO)(1) or the South East Asia Treaty Organization (SEATO)(2). The UGSP recognizes that no single state, on a sustained basis, has the ability to maintain world peace. What follows is the summary of how it will work. The explanation of each of these principles will be detailed in Chapter Seven:

7-1. The UGSP conducts an investigation.

7-2. Any government unable or unwilling to terminate their aggressive actions against another state or eliminate their terrorist cells shall be given the opportunity to immediately surrender their armed forces to the UGSP.

7-3. If UGSP intervention is required, the initial military action must be precise.

7-4. Utilizing the combined intelligence gathering capabilities of UGSP member states, special teams shall eliminate the terrorist cells or "rogue" state leaders.

7-5. The UGSP shall occupy and administer the problem state until the removal of the world threat has been achieved and stabilization has been restored. In some cases this could be years or even generations.

7-6. The UGSP shall determine the form of government each occupied state shall have during occupation. Human rights will be restored and guaranteed. The population shall be made secure.

7-7. The UGSP goal shall be the return to self-rule by the utilization of local administrators and the development of future leaders.

7-8. The UGSP shall ensure that economic and social development shall continue during occupation. This shall be consistent with local values and goals. Where possible, the national development goals will be funded from local industrial and natural resources.

Provisions for the instigation of UGSP action in partnership with the United Nations (UN), the International Court of Justice (ICJ, also known as the World Court and the International Criminal Court (ICC) will be detailed in Chapter Six and subsequent chapters.

CHAPTER ONE

A LOOK AT HISTORY

Beginning a chapter on history with a discussion of the need for dominance may seem strange. However, it is important and relevant.

Through nature's law of natural selection, all animals who have the capability to do so, will dominate others of their kind for breeding rights. Darwin called it "survival of the fittest". This insures biological strengthening of the species. Like any other animal, humans are "hard wired" with the same instinct. However, in humans two very interesting consequences of this instinct occur due to our "superior" brain: 1) humans have the lust not just for "breeding rights", but for territory beyond which any other animal would attempt to control; 2) fortunately humans have developed "socialization" to the point of civilization. This is the coming together of an organized society for the mutual protection from the dangers of unwanted domination.

It is evident from the early anthropological and archeological records that man has been beating each other over the head with clubs or shooting each other with arrows since the dawn of mankind. In primitive times the goal, or necessity, may have been for hunting territory. As we became more sophisticated, the drive for power, possession, and control became more complex. It is interesting that with most animals, the males will mark their territory with their scent. Rarely, if ever, will an animal mark more territory than they can reasonably control. That, to man's folly, is a principle we do not seem to have learned. History has clearly demonstrated that all the great powers have risen to the point where they could no longer sustain their territorial conquests both economically and militarily.(1)

In any undertaking it is important to look carefully at the history of similar circumstances. One must consider the consequences of actions taken, the successes and possibly more importantly, the failures. It has been stated many times that if you do not learn from history you are doomed to repeat history. This is especially true of historical failures. Yet, strangely, as much as this axiom is common knowledge, too often we fail to heed the advice.

Every state in the history of the world has ultimately failed when it has attempted total domination of its sphere of influence. The attempt at total domination has often triggered the decline or doom of many states. It has stretched the military or the economy, or both, to the breaking point. While that may seem so obvious that it need not be mentioned, it is a grave mistake, made over and over again. The United States, in the first half of the twenty-first century is the most powerful state on earth, both economically and militarily. However, the United States is subject to the same fate.

In earlier times, the spread of the Roman Empire beyond that which they could control and the Mongol, Islamic and the European Christian invasions are examples.

At one point the Roman Empire controlled the entire Mediterranean Basin, much of the Mideast, the Iberian Peninsula, most of what is now Europe, including the British Isles. The economic burden of keeping this vast territory under control became too much. The term "economic burden" is here referring to the cost of control in terms of money, manpower and the logistics of the military. The problems with the general supply, the ability to govern and social influence within a given territory became an unmanageable burden. At a point, the Romans could no longer stave off the pressure from other more local groups and maintain their own ambitions for control and expansion.

The Mongols conquered from Eastern Asia through Central Asia and into what is now Eastern Europe. Like the Romans, the Mongols found, to their chagrin, it was too much territory and too much of a burden to control. They, too, were beaten back.

From the late fifteenth century the powers of Europe which included Spain, Portugal, The Netherlands, France and England began to explore and claim vast new unknown territories. These territories included all of the Western Hemisphere, nearly all of Africa, vast territories in the Middle East, Central Asia, Southeast Asia and any other land into which they could place a flag. For a period of time, they exploited to their economic advantage. However, in the attempt to control and to gain at the expense of each other, they warred with each other. In this work it is not important to delve into the various intrigues and alliances. Suffice it to say that each conflict that resulted from their attempts for control led to weakening each of the parties.

Particularly from the eighteenth century on, the "Colonial" powers found it either extremely difficult or impossible to support their empires while threatened with local demands for independence. As an example, the American Revolution was the start of the decline of the British Empire. It is to France's credit that because of their conflicts in Europe and the accompanying economic drain, they realized they could no longer afford the attempt to hold a large portion of their North American territory. Wisely, or with cunning, France sold a vast territory to the United States during the presidency of Thomas Jefferson. That purchase is known as "The Louisiana Purchase". Had France not made that sale, in all likelihood they would have lost it anyway due to the economic inability to defend it against the territorial ambitions of the United States.

In the last few centuries, the demise of the European colonial powers which took Spain, Portugal, The Netherlands, France and England from dominate world powers to the second tier of power is further proof of the folly of unchecked expansion.

Islam, while not a state, spread from what is now Saudi Arabia across a broad swath of land from the African Atlantic coast, the Iberian Peninsula, all the way to present day Indonesia. From the seventh to the fifteenth

3

century Islam was arguably the greatest power on earth. Islam's fall and the variety of causes for the fall are beyond the scope of this work. All of these cases are the seeds of much of today's problems.

Some good twentieth century examples of the presumed need for territory beyond which it was possible to control were Nazi Germany's "Growing Room" and the Soviet Union's military control of their satellite states. The Soviet Union's unsuccessful attempt to spread Communism around the world is another example.

It is amazing in retrospect that Nazi Germany pursued the grand plan of conquest. The Nazis, through propaganda, incited a national attitude of righteous vengeance, intimidation, hard work, and early small conquest. Added to this was the diplomatic capitulation of Great Britain and the seemingly neutral position of the United States. This established Germany as a world power, yet again. However, they failed because they went beyond their capacity to control and supply. That was particularly true when they made the major mistake of invading the Soviet Union. They did not learn the lesson of their "two front" defeat in World War One. They did not have the resources to attempt control over Western Europe, Eastern Europe, parts of Africa and the Soviet Union. Additionally, they did not properly consider the vast military power they were opposing or the outrage that their conduct inspired. This example is not meant as a moral judgment. It is cited merely to illustrate that, as with the Romans, the Mongols and currently with Islamic extremists, no state can control beyond its economic ability to sustain.

States or the alliances of states win wars. The seeds for future conflicts are often planted by the way that war was prosecuted and the way the conquered were treated in the aftermath. World War One is an excellent example. The terms imposed upon Germany by the Treaty of Versailles were so punitive that the resentment ran deep. It was no simple coincidence that the Germans, in the Second World War, forced the French to surrender in the same railway car at Versailles as the French had used for the German surrender in World War One. That World War Two French surrender was a great psychological and propaganda boost to the German people. In part, those terms imposed at the conclusion of World War One and the subsequent economic disaster are why the Nazis were able to gain so much public support from the German people.

The collapse of the Soviet Union is a very interesting example. In the twentieth century, one of the two "superpowers" collapsed without a shot being fired. In any event, few shots. Ultimately, the demise of the Soviet Union can be blamed on a terribly flawed economic system: Communism. A discussion of Communism is not the subject of this work. However, given the ambitions of the Soviet Union, the realities of Communism made it impossible for the Kremlin to economically sustain the military, while trying to provide for the "proletariat", and control and govern regions, "satellites", and states that covered more than eleven times zones of the world's surface. Here again, the historic fact is that no one state can sustain the burden of control over vast territories for an extended period of time.

As stated above, nearly all conflict initially has its origin in dominance: the need by some, almost always initiated by an individual or small group, to have more power, control and/or territory. Some conflicts will be caused by the need for revenge for a past wrong, real or imagined, or for "justice" for a past real or imagined wrong. However, the underlying root cause was, at some point in time, maybe even in the distant past, someone's need for power over another.

What role does religion play in this picture? Scholars argue whether or not the world's religions teach violence and warfare for their own sake. They debate passages in both the Bible and the Koran which advocate violence and other passages which prohibit violence. Many religions do advocate "spreading the word", "the only true God" and creating converts. The preferred method by some practitioners is through the power of verbal and written persuasion. The policies of faiths such as the Mormons and the Seventh Day Adventists are examples. However, too many use the pretext of their religion to wage terrorism and/or war either to create converts or to wipe out dissent. What has this to do with the concept of dominance? Power, and the control of other human beings!

It is a sad commentary on Christianity that the early Church tried so hard to control the minds and the labors of vast populations. This was often done in unison with the state. It was an unholy alliance between the princes of government and the princes of the Church to keep the general population under control. War and terror were used in Europe and in the lands that the Europeans colonized. Through power and dominance there were very few kings, popes or bishops who were anything less than extremely wealthy by the standards of the day.

This need for power led to the suppression of knowledge during the so-called "Dark Ages". There was the dire threat of excommunication for the development and dissemination of new ideas. The Church established the Inquisition which consisted of tribunals to eliminate "heresy". The Church enacted horrific tortures or death to extract confessions or to punish. Galileo was condemned for heresy for his astronomical studies during the Inquisition.

The Church of Rome reached a point in their attempt to control vast masses of people and vast territories that they incited rebellion. We could spend a great deal of time discussing the rise of Protestantism from Martin Luther, Henry the VIII and on. That is not relevant here. What is relevant is that because of the Church's overreaching authoritarianism and the dissention that was thereby created, Protestant rivals were born and are successful to this day. This is a prime example of the principle that says that the way you execute an action today, the way you treat a populace, will plant the seeds of discontent, or goodwill, either in the immediate or distant future.

The Church and the secular governments of Europe inspired and executed the Crusades. While they occurred during the twelfth and thirteenth centuries, the Crusades probably laid the groundwork for much of the Fundamentalist Muslim Arab versus secular European and American conflicts today. It is a credit to the American founding fathers and no accident that they insisted upon the separation of church from state in the creation of the United States.

Many of the late twentieth and early twenty-first century major conflicts in the world have their roots in the Middle East and Southeast Asia. The Israeli/Palestinian conflict and the alliances on both sides certainly play a part, but only a part. Absent that struggle, there would still be major conflicts. Iran and Iraq have warred. Iraq invaded Kuwait and had to have its territorial ambitions checked. The Soviet Union created their own Viet Nam by invading Afghanistan. That adventure drained the resources of the Soviet Union. The tribes and "war lords" of Afghanistan were successful in driving the Soviets out, albeit with clandestine help from the United States. That led to the Taliban takeover of the Afghan government and the providing of a safe haven for al Qaeda. Then, because of the terrorist attacks of al Qaeda, the United States invaded Afghanistan and took down the Taliban regime. What has followed is an extended conflict within Afghanistan, with no end in sight, to attempt to defeat al Qaeda and Taliban terrorism. These actions have not helped the image of the West within the Muslim community.

The legality of the preemptive attacks on Iraq will be argued for some time to come. However, there is no question that it removed an ambitious tyrant. Whether or not Saddam Hussein was a true world threat will never be known. One thing is certain: he was removed before he could be. The legality and the merits of the Iraqi invasion is not the purview of this work. What is relevant for this discussion is the quagmire which resulted from poor planning in the aftermath. That subject will be addressed in Chapter Six and Seven. The reputation of the West has been severely damaged.

Certain individuals, Muslim clerics, and the rulers of certain states, fear losing their power base due to Western influences in the Middle East and Southwest Asia. They have called for "Holy War" or "Jihad" against the United States and its allies. They have called for this "Holy War" under the color of a threat to Islam by the West. Granted, the actions of the West have given some credence to that "us versus them" rhetoric. However, cutting through all the hyperbole and propaganda, a large part of Holy Jihad has to do with the retention or gain of personal power and control.

Historically, despots attempting to gain control will identify a target such as a state, society, ethnic group or religion, and through their propaganda machinery, convince their people of the gross crimes committed against them by that target. It is the "us against them" argument. Most lies have at least a germ of truth in order to be convincing. These are sobering lessons that must be important to the UGSP in the execution of the plan for control and the subsequent administration of those states which are threats to world security.

The quest for world peace is a marvelous political and religious statement, but it never has happened nor will it happen unless mankind faces the fact that we will not live in peace voluntarily. It would appear that it must be enforced by an organized body with the power to do so. States and individuals recoil at that thought while they lament the continued occurrence of violence. This idea of a world police force is antithetical to states because no state will be willing to give up an element of their sovereignty. Yet, no one would dream of a city without a police force. The world should recognize that it is no different.

This work will be discussing at great length the premise that all conflicts start with an individual or small group. If recognized early on, that individual or group could be managed or dealt with before the problem gets out of control. In the First Edition of this book written in 2001 it was stated that the so-called "Muslim Extremists" and the leaders such as Iraq's Saddam Hussein were still of a problem size that could have been controlled. Saddam is gone, but unfortunately, Muslim Extremism is no longer a small problem. It must be emphasized that some observers state there is no correlation between "Muslim Extremist" and the basic principles of Islam. Other observers disagree. The civilized world had better not let the problem grow any larger because there are millions of people, under the guise of Islam, being influenced by these extremists who are creating an armed conflict of major world destabilizing proportions.

The United States cannot impose its will with respect to the eradication of terrorism worldwide without major help and cooperation from its allies and, in some cases, its potential foes. The United States cannot do it alone militarily, economically, administratively or in the court of world opinion. Sadly, the United States appears to be ignoring the lessons of history. While some states are rendering support, the United States appears to be too confident of its abilities and is therefore assuming too much of the burden of enforcing world order. The attitude seems to be that the United States is the only state with the capability therefore it must be the world's "policeman".

In the "Letter to the Editor" which started the Preface to this work, this author mentioned careful diplomacy and a soft military handling of zealots. In short, appeasement. More benignly, looking the other way and/or hoping the problem will go away or solve itself is another example. Those principles do not work. In the mid 1930's, had the Allies taken a much stronger stance instead of trying to negotiate with Nazi Germany, they might have prevented that European war. If the Allies had not all but ignored Japanese advances in Asia and had the United States ceased selling the Japanese raw material, they might have so limited Japanese strength that Pearl Harbor might never have happened. Granted, after World War One, the United States was in an isolationist mood. In the 1930's, the rest of the world and the United States were trying to struggle back from a worldwide depression. The United States needed all the markets it could get. Nonetheless, the point of not facing the problem is still valid.

As in most aspects of life, it is better to solve the problem while it is still of a manageable size than find yourself in a position where the problem is out of control and the consequences far more severe. Today's regional problems and the terrorist threat are glaring examples of the validity of this philosophy for the prevention of a potential calamity.

When a state or a people have suffered a horrific act such as happened to the United States on September 11, 2001, in their anger and their known military might, there are strong emotions to strike back immediately and massively. Given the above lessons, that would solidify the hatred in the Middle East for the "Great Satan", and it would come back to haunt the United States for years to come. It would give ammunition to those who would vilify the United States. It would thereby convince some people who originally did not hate the United States that, in fact, the United States is the "Great Satan".

The crisis response of the UGSP and its plan must be measured and sure. It is time to again recognize that no one state can do it alone. It is time to recognize that the coalitions that have been formed to meet various conflicts must evolve into a permanent organization. The proposed UGSP would not only put a stop to the terrorists but would also put into place a reconstruction plan that would work to change the attitudes in the region. It would work to "win the hearts and minds" in the region. It is time to form the United Global Security Partnership.

CHAPTER TWO

THREATS TO WORLD PEACE AND SECURITY

During the American Revolution the British complained bitterly that the Americans did not fight "like gentlemen". They hid behind trees instead of in rows where the front row knelt and fired, moved back to reload while the second row moved forward, knelt and fired. That war and many subsequent wars had those "line up the troops and mow them down" tactics. Guerilla warfare, though not new, was successfully employed by the American Revolutionaries. That required new security measures for which the British did not understand nor use.

World War One saw the introduction of the "aeroplane" and up until that time the greatest use of mechanized warfare. It also saw the introduction of chemical warfare on a large scale. Biological warfare, which has been around since antiquity, was also employed. The Geneva Protocol of 1925 prohibited the use of chemical and biological agents in warfare.(1) That prohibition has been constantly violated.

World War Two ushered in massive sea power, long range bombers, the jet engine and missiles such as the German ME-262 jets and the V1 and V2 rockets, radar and the atomic bomb. World War Two also helped perfect intelligence gathering and special strike teams. Radar, intelligence gathering, aerial and seaborne surveillance were security outgrowths of that war.

World War Two also ushered in the atomic age with the United States' use of the atomic bomb on Japan. By 1947 the Soviet Union also had "the bomb". The United States countered with the hydrogen bomb. The arms race was on! With this race came rapid advances in technology including ICBMs and multiple warheads and the nuclear submarine. The arms build-up was massive and frightening. All of this culminated in treaties which created "assured mutual destruction". Nuclear superpowers had created the threat of a world annihilating form of the old military tactic of "line up the troops and mow them down".

The arms build-up immediately became referred to as the "Cold War". Beginning right after World War Two, it did not end until the collapse of the Soviet Union in 1991. The primary adversaries were the "Western Allies", led by the United States, verses the "Eastern Block", led by the Soviet Union. While they had their own tensions, the Soviet Union and China were allied. The Cold War, with its massive build-up of world-destroying arms, created considerable world stress and unrest.

Analyzing the Cold War is extremely important in formulating a plan for world security here at the beginning of the twenty-first century. Why? Because it still clouds our thinking.

To understand the Cold War, one must be acquainted with some Russian history. The 1917 Revolution was fought to overthrow centuries of czarist oppression. Vladimir Lenin and the Bolsheviks used the czarist oppression of the people, making the Czar the target, to win the public support in the Bolshevik quest for power. Interestingly, just as Czar Peter the Great used state terrorism, Lenin often spoke of terrorism's need in consolidating one's power. Then Joseph Stalin raised state terrorism to an art form.

The Bolsheviks used the "Utopian" ideas of a classless, worker's paradise embodied in Marxist Communism to win the "hearts and minds" of the Russian people. Communism is not a form of government. It is an economic theory. That theory requires government control, a "dictatorship of the proletariat", until it matures into a self-supporting institution. It was never used in its pure form by Lenin, Stalin or their successors. Communism's bastardized use was a tool for control of the people by giving a false sense of hope and by state control of the ownership of all resources. For much of seventy years those controls allowed the Soviet Union to become a major world power. Russia intimidated, "protected", or defeated surrounding states in the 1920's, thus forming the Soviet Union. Stalin further expanded the Soviet Union with the "satellite" states acquired as spoils after World War Two. The Soviet Union then set about keeping the pressure on the West in Soviet Union's quest to spread Communism around the world.

Because of the vastly different ideologies and ambitions, the seeds of adversity between the Soviet Union and the West, or Free World, were sown long before World War Two. The Soviets feared the West and the West feared the Soviets. Much of the Soviet paranoia was based on the fact that every invasion of their territory for the last thousand years had come from the West. The West's very credible fear was the threat to democratic institutions by the Soviet ambitions.

There was a strange sense of security brought about by the Cold War. First, we all knew who the enemy was and second, because of the assured mass mutual destruction, it was and still is believed that nobody would be foolish enough to start such a conflagration. Unfortunately, in 2014/2015 Russia annexed Ukrainian Crimea, threatened Eastern Ukraine and other parts of Eastern Europe. Therefore, the mutual distrust still drives much of East/West foreign policy.

Beginning in 1950, during the Cold War, North Korea invaded South Korea. From a world security standpoint, the Korean "police action" demonstrated the "free world" was willing to meet aggression with force. When the Soviet Union walked out of the United Nations debate on the invasion of South Korea by North Korea, the UN was able to put together a coalition, led by the United States, to stop the North Korean aggression.

With the Soviet Union's delegation walk out of the UN Security Council proceedings, they forfeited their ability to exercise their veto power.

As one of the five permanent members of the Security Council, by default, the Soviets unwittingly allowed the UN to check North Korean aggression.

The Korean Conflict created great advances in jet aircraft. The helicopter was introduced as new tool of modern warfare.

The Korean conflict was a stalemate ending in 1953. North Korea and South Korea have never signed a peace treaty. Technically, the Korean conflict has not ended. North Korea continues to threaten South Korea which is causing the Korean Peninsula to be an armed camp. There are constant threats, counter-threats, displays of military might between the North and the South and endless negotiations. This is an excellent example of the difficulties of diplomacy in solving international conflicts.

During the long Viet Nam conflict the helicopter gunship was widely used. That allowed for an enormous increase in the ability to insert and extract troops and to strike quickly. Vietnam saw the return to guerilla warfare on a large scale. It was very successfully employed against the United States by the forces of the Viet Cong and the North Vietnamese.

The United States, it's allies and, therefore, South Vietnam, lost! The United States lost for a variety of reasons. With all of its military might, the United States did not have a clear purpose. Without that clear purpose the United States did not have the full support of the American people. Additionally, Vietnam ushered in the greatest increase in media coverage of any war in history. Americans watching the "Evening News" on television witnessed the cost of that unrelenting guerilla warfare in American lives. Americans were to a large degree demoralized. As Marshall McLuhan said, "The war in Viet Nam was lost in the living rooms of America, not on the battlefields of Viet Nam." The United States did not have the support of much of the world. The United States feared the wrath of its two greatest adversaries, the Soviet Union and China, if the United States "over-employed" its massive military might.

For all states, not just the United States, Vietnam presents some of the greatest lessons in achieving international security in today's world. While the ideologies of that conflict and today's terrorist threat may be different, the following lessons are of the utmost importance:

1: Never enter a conflict without a clear purpose, plan and goal.
2: Be sure your intelligence is first rate.
3: Secure the help, cooperation and understanding of your allies. Show the rest of the world that your actions will either not harm their interest or, in fact will be in their best long-term interest. At the very least, other states must be convinced that their interference or opposition would not be in their best interest.

The purpose of highlighting prior wars and their technological advances is to illustrate that the nature of world security threats and the means to combat them are ever-evolving. This puts enormous pressure and expense on states to stay abreast of, or ahead of, the challenges.

The world has changed. When the Soviet Union finally failed in 1991 it was reduced to the "third world" economic status that, in reality, it had been for some time. Each of the Soviet Union's member states and the "satellite" states gained their independence. Those states have gone their separate ways while still maintaining economic association with the Russian Federation. Some of those states, of course, are doing better than others. For example, the Baltic States, Poland and Hungary are generally faring well. Ukraine was holding its own until the Russian annexation of the Crimea and the Russian support of Eastern Ukrainian separatists. East Germany was reunited with West Germany in 1990. However, many of the states have serious problems, both economic and political. Georgia has faced rebel factions using terrorist tactics. Both Georgia and the Russian Federation were affected by problems in Chechnya, and that conflict was in danger of spreading. Chechnya both imported and exported militant terrorist fighters. Armenia and Azerbaijan have quarreled. The other states that border Southwest Asia such as Kazakhstan, Turkmenistan, Uzbekistan and Kirghizia are desperately poor, and the Russian Federation fears the influence of factions within the bordering Middle Eastern and Southwest Asian states. The Russian Federation has been struggling for its economic survival and with caution and suspicion, has turned to the West for economic help. The West must do all it can do, with honesty, to build a trust and partnership. However, Russia has regained much of its power and influence.

This work has stated that the Cold War mentality still clouds our thinking. In some quarters we still think in terms of multiple missiles flying. Hopefully, Russia will modify its 2015 behavior and not become the threat it once presented. If they will make that change, the Russian Federation has worlds to gain by working with the West, and they should know it.

No other power in the world has the ability YET, to threaten the world with global reaching strategic missiles other than the United States, Russia, the United Kingdom, France, China, India, Pakistan, and with North Korea and possibly Iran coming on. Part of the United States' security strategy was to develop an "anti-missile shield". While that may have merit, the plan that will be presented for the United Global Security Partnership in this work may negate that necessity.

In addition to the above, in the beginning of the twenty-first century we find there are other threats to world peace and security.

India and Pakistan both have nuclear weapons, and they are feuding. India is accusing Pakistan of exporting terrorism to India in their dispute over control of the Kashmir region. Both sides have expressed their willingness to use their nuclear weapons.

There are some growing threats from countries such as Iran and North Korea which are working diligently to develop their capability with nuclear, chemical and biological weapons. Iran is characterized as the world's leading exporter of terrorism. The world should not allow this threat to continue because, as history has shown us, we should pay now or we will pay a much greater price later.

In today's world the real threat to world peace and security also includes the regional conflicts that spread into neighboring areas such as the problems in the Balkans, Africa, India/Pakistan, Afghanistan, Iraq, Syria and the Israeli/Palestinian conflict. World peace and security is also seriously threatened by the small fanatical groups which use regional conflicts and religion as excuses to target states as enemies and employ terrorist tactics to inflict harm and damage. This terrorist-targeting is by no means limited to victimizing the United States.

With the break-up of the Soviet Union and the poor controls employed by the Russian Federation over their military inventory, much of the military hardware is unaccounted for, and therefore, cannot be located. Further, because of their late twentieth century and early twenty-first century history of poor economic conditions, unpaid military, unpaid or underpaid scientists managers and technicians, much of their military equipment and technology, including nuclear, has being sold on the "black market". Cash strapped states such as the Russian Federation and North Korea sell advanced technology indiscriminately.

The United States is probably the largest arms supplier in the world. Other major arms suppliers include the United Kingdom, Germany and France. All international arms suppliers need to be more constrained in their arms sales. Much of that armament has come into the hands of the various terrorist groups.

With the advances in technology, it will not be necessary to use a missile to deliver nuclear, chemical or biological weapons. A suitcase may do quite nicely. In most of the free world, access to borders and major civilian and military targets is relatively easy. September 11, 2001 proved that fact graphically. This should be of grave concern to the free world, indeed, the entire world, and a cause for developing and implementing the United Global Security Partnership.

CHAPTER THREE

THE JUSTIFICATION AND PRECEDENCE FOR THE UNITED GLOBAL SECURITY PARTNERSHIP

In Chapter One, "A Look At History", it was stated that there always have been and there always will be individuals or small groups with unreasonable ambitions which will create conflicts. That is the justification for the formation of the UGSP to enforce world peace. As stated, man has never nor ever will live in peace voluntarily.

Sometimes International Law has helped. There are two basic concepts in International Law. International Law is either "codified" in the form of treaties, or "customary" in the form of precedence.(1) While well intentioned, there are many problems in International Law. Because of the multitude of laws, many of the principles are contradictory. However, the most important difficulty is that International Law has no enforcement vehicle. With "Domestic Law", that is law within a state, the decisions of a court are enforceable by a police force. Not so with International Law. Adherence is voluntary. Even with codified treaties, any party to a treaty can, and sometimes does, declare that they are no longer bound by that treaty.

There is an International Court of Justice (ICJ), more commonly known as the World Court.(2) It is the court for the UN and is designed to settle disputes between states. Because appearance before the court is voluntary and its decisions are largely unenforceable, the ICJ acts more like a mediator or an arbitrator.

For the resolution of violent conflict, there is the International Criminal Court (ICC).(3) It does have the power of arrest and imprisonment. However, there are major shortcomings. First, states must agree to allow their citizens to be subject to the court. The United States, for example, refuses to allow American citizens to be prosecuted by the ICC. Second, to date, the ICC only has jurisdiction against individuals, not states.

Most people and most states find the notion of a global police force reprehensible. That fact is the single most prominent obstacle to the formation of the UGSP. It is why, dating from the League of Nations to the present, even though the concept has been debated no credible international police force has yet been formed. Interestingly, however, no state has a problem with the concept of a city, state or national police force, and in fact, all states demand them. This is precedence and it should be recognized that on a larger scale, the world is no different from a city in controlling uncivilized members of society.

A way must be found to mitigate the problem of the violation of sovereignty. The sovereignty and sanctity of any state would not be threatened by a UGSP unless that state has become a demonstrated threat to world security. History, both past and recent, provide both the justification and the precedence for the formation of the UGSP. One would hope the world is paying attention.

The catastrophic results of the September 11, 2001 terrorist attack on the United States was a wake-up call. Suddenly, the entire world realized that if it could happen in the United States with such a horrific outcome, it could happen anywhere. Many of the states of the world have suffered terrorist attacks. All understand that given the fanatical nature of terrorist attacks, they are very difficult to prevent. If a suicide bomber wants to walk into a public place, or drive a car bomb, or fly an airplane loaded with fuel into a public place, there is very little law enforcement or a state's military can do to stop them. That is unless, through intelligence gathering, states get very lucky. The same will be true of low yield nuclear devices planted at power stations, transportation hubs or military installations. The same can be said for poisoning a water supply with chemical or biological weapons. The list and methods are as long as one's imagination. The whole world knows this, as do both the perpetrators and the potential victims. Along with small regional conflicts in which terrorism will be employed, "Lone Wolf" attacks (individuals acting alone) and terrorist "cells" (small groups) are the ways many wars will be fought for the foreseeable future. Relatively speaking, it is inexpensive warfare, and even the smallest of groups can succeed to some measure. It is also a method that most terrorist groups believe will make a political or religious statement. This is not to say that state to state warfare or intrastate conflict will no longer occur. They most certainly will.

No terrorist group or government suddenly becomes a world threat. Granted, a terrorist group may first come to world attention as a result of a violent act on their part. However, they do start small as a manageable threat. Similarly, political regimes with world mischief in mind, could be controlled or countered in their early stages. Most of these groups give us early warning if we would pay attention. It often comes in the form of rhetoric and bitter tirades. Therefore, only the most naive or wishful thinking among us can fail to realize the dangerous intentions in the early stages of the development of these groups or governments. As has been said before in this work and will be said again, it is far better to solve a problem in its early stages while it is still manageable than after it has become a large problem which has spun out of control.

Historically, these are major points and lessons of allowing a problem to grow:

1: The United States and the West, along with other peace loving states of the world, are reluctant to become engaged in conflicts.

2: The United States and the West are too concerned about world opinion, often from quarters which will oppose them in any event.

3: The United States and the West allow their hope that ambitious governments will act responsibly to cloud their judgment.

4: The United States and the West must recognize that terrorist groups acting violently are an increasing threat and must be dealt with decisively.

5: Appeasement does not work. The failed attempts at appeasement with Nazi Germany prove the point. It could be argued that the huge cost, in lives and resources, of World War Two might have been prevented had early intervention had been taken.

In the last one hundred years there is ample justification and precedence for the establishment of the UGSP. Sadly, as argued in this work, the alliances and coalitions to stop aggression have been formed too late in some cases to stop the huge cost in lives and resources. At the conclusion of the action or war, the alliance has either dissolved, become loose knit, or if permanent, lacked the will or the power to gear up again without a tremendous effort, diplomacy and, in some cases, a loss in strategic advantage. That has allowed the inevitable development of problem situations.

However, there have been some successes. For example, the formation of the North Atlantic Treaty Organization (NATO)(4) may have prevented threats to Western Europe during the Cold War years. The UN forces in Korea, led by the United States, prevented the disappearance of South Korea as an independent state. The UN "peacekeeping" forces at various times and places around the world has, in some cases, limited or stopped a conflict. Unfortunately, in many cases it has not.

In recent times, the coalition led by the United States that checked Iraq's incursion into Kuwait in 1991 was very successful. These actions on the part of cooperating states are certainly precedence for the formation of the United Global Security Partnership.

One could argue that such a partnership is not necessary because the world has the UN and security organizations such as NATO and (SEATO).(5)

That argument will be examined in the next chapter. Even with the shortcomings of the UN, NATO and SEATO, these organizations give precedence for the formation of the UGSP.

It is interesting that there are many quarters that believed the "Gulf War Coalition" should have continued that 1991 war and removed the regime of Saddam Hussein in Iraq. Many governments viewed that regime as a continuing world threat and a supporter of worldwide terrorism. Indeed, Iraq in 2001 was an excellent example of the need and justification for the formation of the UGSP. It was known that within his own borders, Saddam Hussein had killed many people who he believed opposed his rule. He thereby demonstrated his lack of concern for human life. Witness his abortive attempt to expand his influence and his borders by his attack on Kuwait.

Nearly all of the intelligence organizations around the world believed Saddam was building chemical and biological weapons and expanding attempts to develop atomic weapons with the missile ability to strike. Critics of the Iraq invasion of 2003 point out that weapons of mass destruction were never found and, therefore, the invasion was unwarranted and illegal. No weapons of mass destruction? Ask the gassed Kurds in the north and the Shiite Muslims in the south. Is there anyone so naive as to believe that if, in fact, Saddam was developing further weapons of mass destruction, he would not have employed them to disrupt the world order and security?

The "sanctions" imposed on Iraq by the UN were being violated and were largely ineffectual. The United States interpreted some of the provisions of the resolutions for those sanctions to justify the 2003 invasion of Iraq and the removal of Saddam Hussein.

If ever there was a legitimate rationale for a UGSP, a global policeman, composed of responsible global powers, Iraq's aggressive actions were ample justification. It was not about religion. It was not about ethnicity. It was about one man's ambitions, along with colleagues, and the desire to dominate with the ultimate unnecessary loss of human life and the unnecessary expenditures of vast resources.

If the UGSP can be credible, the political fallout will be potentially a much more manageable problem than the violent problem which will surely come if, as in this example, Iraq had been allowed to pursue its ambitions. Unfortunately, in the case of Iraq, the planning of the aftermath and a clear understanding of the culture was not well considered. The inbred conflict between Sunni and Shiite Islam and inter-tribal strife either were not understood or they were ignored. With proper planning the principle holds: cure the problem while it is small and manageable or face the demon when it is out of control.

It has already been stated that no one state, no matter how strong it may be both economically and militarily, would be able to secure and maintain world peace by itself. Regardless of how altruistic that state's motives and actions may be, trying to maintain world order could be viewed as a form of world domination. History has shown time and again that the sustained drain on that state's, or empire's, resources has reduced that state to the second or third tier of world powers.(6) Today, because such a control would be worldwide rather than regional as in past centuries, the enormous economic and military resources required would in time ruin even the most powerful of states.

There is another very important reason why no one state could enforce world peace on its own. That is the court of world opinion. Again, even though the motives may be altruistic, very few states would accept the domination of one power. Most states would see that domination as a threat to their security and their sovereignty. This is the position in which the United States finds itself in the early decades of the twenty-first century. It matters not that the United States is one of the greatest providers of world aid. When the United States believes it necessary to flex its muscle and/or exert its influence, much of the world views those actions as a form of aggression or an attempt to dominate. Yet, the very survival of civilized man cries out for the need of some form of control of rogue states, rogue groups and rogue individuals.

As stated above, almost no one objects to the establishment of police forces in towns and cities around the world. That acceptance is based on the agreement between government and the citizenry that the police force is there to protect the citizenry from violence and provide safety. That acceptance is not there when the police force is a political enforcement arm of the ruling government. The world should be no different. The world needs a global police force. A police force free of politics or ambitions. The UGSP could be that police force.

The idea of a world "policeman" is an unpopular concept with most of the people and the states of the world. There are fears as to sovereignty and domination. There are justified fears of favoritism and exploitation by a power or a group of powers which are capable of exercising military control. These are strong arguments against the formation of a UGSP. At the outset this author will agree that one would not be able to win total world acceptance to such an idea. If that total acceptance were considered possible, it is conceivable that the world would already have a UGSP. However, there are ways to make it tolerable in its initial stages. Long term acceptance will be achieved through the UGSP's "blind" adherence to justice and its "even handed" approach to world security.

In the meantime, unfortunately, the world continues to be plagued with crisis after crisis. Any one of these crises could lead to world disaster.

CHAPTER FOUR

THE FAILURES OF THE UNITED NATIONS(1)

The twentieth century was the bloodiest century in the history of humankind. The violence continues at the beginning of the twenty-first century. The UN has been a major factor in world affairs for the last seventy years of the carnage. Why, given the stated goals, has the UN sustained such a poor record of maintaining peace and security in the world? The answer to that question presents profound political and International Law questions and challenges.

The Charter of the United Nations was signed on June 28, 1945 for the purpose of maintaining world peace and security. The Preamble to the Charter sets out the goals envisioned by the founding members.(2)   For our purposes the most important passages include: "…to save succeeding generations from the scourge of war,…"; "…to unite our strength to maintain international peace and security…"; and, "…that armed force shall not be used, save in the common interest,…". In short, *ostensibly* the UN was founded on the principles of achieving peace and maintaining security. To that end the United Nations has failed.

Article 1.1 states, "To maintain international peace and security, and to that end: to take effective collective measures for the prevention and removal of threats to the peace, and for the suppression of acts of aggression or other breaches of the peace, and to bring about by peaceful means, and in conformity with the principles of justice and International Law, adjustments or settlements of international disputes or situations which might lead to a breach of the peace;".

Let us consider the basic premise that the founding was based on peace and security. This author used the phraseology "*ostensibly*...founded on the principles of achieving peace and maintaining security..." However, was it really? Not if one believes Antonio Cassese's summation of the positions of Stalin and Roosevelt.(3) According to Cassese, Stalin is reported to have noted, "...the main thing was to prevent quarrels in the future between the three Great Powers, (USA, Britain and the USSR) and the task, therefore, was to secure their unity for the future..." Cassese states that Roosevelt "fully shared that view". If this is true, one could argue that the true founding of the United Nations was to *maintain the peace and security of the Allied Powers* and without necessarily a concern for the world at large. Cassese tells us that Roosevelt envisioned the Security Council as the "board of directors of the world" responsible for "enforcing the peace against any potential miscreant". One could easily read into that premise that the Allied Powers saw the UN as a vehicle to maintain the postwar status quo. It could be argued that this envisioned status quo could have remained, but the Great Powers' cooperation came apart with the onset of the Cold War and the dividing of the world into two opposing camps: the West, headed by the United States; and the Eastern Bloc, headed by the Soviet Union.

If the premise regarding maintaining the post-war status quo is true, it is possible that the Allied Powers, through the vehicle of the UN, believed they could control world peace and order. The establishment of the Security Council gave the Allied Powers their "board of directors for the world". However, they may have believed that to lend credibility to the Security Council, it needed to have more members than just the five *permanent members* (the United States, Great Britain, France, the USSR and, later, China). Therefore, Article 23 creates a Security Council consisting of fifteen members, ten *non-permanent members* in addition to the five permanent members.(4)

Article 42 allows for military intervention by stating, "Should the Security Council consider that measures provided for in Article 41 would be inadequate or have proven to be inadequate, it may take such action by air, sea or land forces as may be necessary to maintain or restore international peace and security. Such actions may include demonstrations, blockage, and other operations by air, sea or land forces of Members of the United Nations."(5)

Yet, since its formation, there have been over 170 major conflicts for which the UN has taken immediate action on only two occasions.(6) The first was the invasion of South Korea in June of 1950. That action was approved by the Security Council only because the Soviet Union's delegation walked out of the debate and, therefore did not vote. It was a mistake the Soviet Union would never make again. The second action was the expulsion of Iraqi forces from Kuwait in 1991. Even then, the Security Council only gave acknowledgement of the legality of the United States coalition.

A large part of the problem is the result of the VETO power in the Security Council which is held by the five permanent members of the Security Council; the United States, Russia, The United Kingdom, France and China. It is difficult, at best, to arrive at a consensus to stop threats to world security or put an end to a conflict. Too many Security Council member states have conflicting interests.

In order for a Security Council resolution to pass, nine of the members must vote in the affirmative and, according to Article 27.3, that vote *must* include the "...concurring votes of the permanent members..."(7) Article 27.3 becomes the source of the VETO. While not specifically using the term *veto*, "*concurring votes*" has been taken to mean the granting of a *veto power* individually to each of the five permanent members. That veto power has often proved to be crippling for UN *peace-making* and *peace-keeping* efforts throughout its existence.

During the negotiations for the drafting of the UN Charter each of the Allied Powers wanted to ensure that each of them could always protect their vital interest and, therefore, insisted upon a veto power. Even if the Cold War had never developed, how could the Allied Powers, given their different political philosophies, have been so short-sighted as to not realize that one or more of their vital interest would likely be involved in nearly all world conflicts? Maybe they were not so short-sighted. It appears they recognized the political nature of world conflict and their vital interest involvement and, therefore, they created a "kill switch", a unilateral tool to defeat a disagreeable resolution.

Whatever the reason, the protection of vital interest being the most logical, the veto power has very likely been the single cause most responsible for the inability of the UN to be truly effective in maintaining world peace and security. This presents an enormous political problem and a question for effective International Law in curbing violence in the world. This author's premise is that to be an effective instrument of International Law in the controlling of world violence the UN must do something to either restrict or eliminate the veto power. This may be an impossible task. By virtue of the fact that the permanent members' vital interests are at stake, it is highly unlikely that they would vote to restrict that protection. Given the structure of the UN, no substantive action can be taken, including amending the United Nations Charter, without the concurrence of the permanent members of the Security Council.

Closely associated with the veto power is the problem of the highly political nature of most of the resolutions by the Security Council for action, or inaction, in the maintenance of international peace and security. Craig J. Barker states that, "The Security Council is undoubtedly an inherently political organ which is arguably incapable of making legal determinations of this manner."(8) Barker is referring to determining when a threat to world peace has gone too far. Why is a decision made to take action in one situation while no action is approved in another situation with similar circumstances?

Why Kosovo, even though a NATO action, and not Rwanda? Some scholars allege that the defining motivation involves the degree of importance associated with the problem area to the world. More specifically, how important is the region to the vital interest of one or more of the permanent members of the Security Council? A major challenge and question for the fairness of International Law and the UN role in maintaining peace and security is the removal of politics and the establishment of objectivity in the enforcement of peace and security. Needless to say, this is a tall order. While removing politics from the process may be nearly impossible, efforts could be made to work toward a uniformity of enforcement policies.

Lastly, with respect to the veto power and the role of politics in the controlling of *international* and *intra-state* violence, is the UN fatally flawed? Or, has the time come when the UN needs to make an honest appraisal of its policies and procedures? Should the UN establish a working commission to attempt to objectively appraise the UN's record of successes and failures, its rules, procedures and objectives in a changing world and, therefore, recommend appropriate structural changes based on those findings to the UN as a whole?

It could be argued that the complications of International Law with respect to intervention in conflict either makes consensus to act difficult or provides a rationale for states to object to intervention. In this author's view there was a glaring example of the use of interpretation of International Law as a rationale for UN non-action. During the Darfur massacres in Sudan, Kofi Annan, the then Secretary General of the United Nations, was interviewed on CNN. Paraphrased, he stated, "We must be careful in calling it genocide because to do so would require action."

NATO is probably as close as we have come to a security partnership. Unfortunately, its scope is not worldwide. NATO is more responsive than proactive. Although, in recent times NATO has taken a more aggressive stance than the UN. Article 5 of NATO's charter, "An attack against one is an attack against all." is important regarding a reaction to aggression against a member state.(9) It does precious little to prevent the problem before it becomes too great. In fact, the events of September 11, 2001 is the first time NATO has invoked that doctrine. To its credit, however, NATO has sent forces to places such as the Balkans to contain a conflict before it becomes a worldwide problem.

SEATO has the same organizational problem that we find in NATO. That is, SEATO is responsive rather than proactive.(10) SEATO, like NATO, has the problem of being regional rather than worldwide.

As precedence for the formation of the UGSP, one should look very closely at both NATO and SEATO. The basic structures of NATO and SEATO could very possibly become the foundation of the UGSP. As argued in this work, the scope must be expanded to encompass the entire world and the organization must be very proactive. It should include those states who are serious about world order and have the will and the ability to insure world security.

Should the UN be abandoned? Certainly not! However, its responsibilities are too great. There are only so many tasks one organization can do well. With its great number of member states, the UN should focus on its humanitarian efforts and not try to be the" world's policeman". The role of the "world's policeman" should be vested in an independent agency, the UGSP. However, the caveat would be that the UN "peacekeeping" role would continue where needed after the initial intervention in a conflict by the UGSP.

CHAPTER FIVE

THE TREATMENT OF SOVEREIGNTY, AGGRESSION, AND INTERVENTION(1)

It is obvious that International Law designed to control violent conflict is built around the concepts of *sovereignty*, *aggression*, and *intervention*. There are certainly disagreements as to the definitions of these concepts. An over simplified description of sovereignty would be the right of a state to conduct its own affairs without the interference from another state. It also provides for the sanctity of a state's territorial boundaries. Aggression could be described as a state's violation of the sovereignty of another state. Such aggression could be military, economic or even targeted propaganda. Intra-state aggression could be internal violence against that state's citizens. Intervention involves a state's or group of states' interference, usually associated with a violent situation occurring between other states. It might also be the interference with a state's or group of states' acts of genocide or gross violations of human rights.

An explanation of *Primary* and *Secondary* laws is in order. A Primary Law is a basic principle such as "thou shalt not kill". Secondary Laws are those which provide for the implementation, interpretation, enforcement, and the criteria for the amendment of the Primary Law.

This chapter will demonstrate the insufficiencies of Primary Law. Primary Law most often lacks supporting institutions which are provided by Secondary Laws or Rules. In the literature "Secondary Laws" are often referred to as "Secondary Rules". The result is a great handicap for enforcement. There are concerns for sovereignty. What acts constitute aggression and the legality of intervention? These questions cause Primary International Law to be ambiguous without Secondary Law clarification and thus fostering inappropriate action or inaction.

Codified Law is written law including treaties. *Customary Law* is unwritten but is established by precedence. In the last chapter there was a discussion regarding the failure of the UN. It should become clear in this chapter that a major part of the problem is the ambiguity of International Law. In part, this ambiguity could be attributed to contradictory Codified and Customary Law which allow states to interpret almost as they wish to protect their national interest. Therefore, consensus on a course of action is often impossible in matters of conflict resolution.

SOVEREIGNTY

In today's world, the issue of sovereignty becomes more complex and critical from a world security perspective. Of interest to this author is the degree to which a state's government jeopardizes, in whole or in part, its sovereignty through acts of unconventional aggression. These include the increasing problems of terrorism, genocide, the broad scope of human rights violations, and civil conflict. They also include states' direct or indirect support of those acts.

"What then is sovereignty? To say that a state is sovereign means that it decides for itself how to cope with its internal and external problems, including whether or not to seek assistance from others"(2) This quote of Kenneth Waltz is by no means a definition of sovereignty. It is a description of one of the features of sovereignty. It is germane to this discussion because it gets to the heart of the issue of the rights of the international community, or lack thereof, to intervene in the affairs of states. This is important with respect to aggression and its potential effect on the international community.

The UN Charter sanctifies the notion of state's sovereignty. It does so in Article 2.1 which states, "The Organization is based on the principle of the sovereign equality of all its Members." Article 2.4 goes on by stating in part, "All Members shall refrain in their international relations from the threat or use of force against the territorial integrity or political independence of any state...." Sub-paragraph Seven (Art. 2.7) is even more direct, "Nothing contained in the present Charter shall authorize the United Nations to intervene in matters which are essentially within the domestic jurisdiction of any state...."(3)

Article 2.1 sets the stage. It declares that the UN is founded on the idea of the sovereign equality of all its members. It is the declaration of a principle or a general guide. Article 2.4 is a Primary Law. However, it becomes ambiguous because it lacks Secondary Rules clarifying, for example, the meaning of the word "refrain". Does it mean never, or are there circumstances when sovereignty can be breached and force is permissible? Nor are there Secondary Rules for a breach of this Article. Article 2.7, a Primary Law, shares the same problems. There are no Secondary Rules defining those matters which are essentially within the domestic jurisdiction. There are no Secondary Rules governing breaches of this Article. These problems of Primary and Secondary Law become important because states are left to interpret these Articles as suits their national interests. Additionally, these insufficiencies often create, in times of crisis, endless debate resulting in inappropriate action, delayed action or no action.

The principle of the sanctity of sovereignty has long been a principle in traditional International Law and, indeed, in modern International Law. However, many scholars differ as to the extent of the sanctity of sovereignty. Some thinkers have reservations as to the actual sanctity of sovereignty. Thomas Hobbes described international relations as a "state of war" of all against all. Hobbes further believed that states are free to pursue their individual goals in relation to other states without moral or legal restrictions.(4) As opposed to the Hobbesian anarchy, Grotius said that all states, in their dealings with one another, are bound by the rules and institutions of the society they form. They are bound not only by rules of prudence or expediency but also by imperatives of morality and law.(5) Vattel (1758), in his work "The Law of Nations", states that the law of nations is the science of the rights which exist between states, and the obligations corresponding to these rights.(6) These reservations with respect to the sanctity of sovereignty become important for consideration of the control of twenty-first century violence.

Since the turn of the twentieth century, but more particularly since the end of the Second World War, in the West there has been a growing awareness of human rights and the realization of the need to protect those rights. This has had a profound effect on how states, institutions, and thinkers view the sanctity of sovereignty. This means that there has been a growing acceptance of the norm that sovereignty includes responsibilities.

Under traditional International Law states could very well do as they pleased, including aggressively intervening in the internal affairs of other states.(7) That would imply that the sanctity of sovereignty was reserved for the powerful and that sanctity is somewhat tenuous for the not so powerful. The UN Charter attempts to mitigate the ability of the powerful to aggressively intervene in the affairs of the not so powerful with the Primary Law for the respect for sovereignty in Article 2.4. It also makes this attempt by appointing itself as the sole determiner of a breach of the peace in Article 39 and as the sole authority for the use of force in Article 42. Unfortunately, because of the lack of Secondary Rules to interpret Article 39 which should outline acts which constitute a "…threat to the peace, breach of the peace, or act of aggression…", the powerful make their own interpretations. Therefore, they retain the ability to breach the sovereignty of the not so powerful when it either suits their national interests or out of frustrations for the endless UN debates and the lack of ensuing direction.

Former United Nations Secretary General Javier Perez de Cuellar stated, "I have no doubt that a major challenge for the U[nited] N[ations] in the future will be to find the right balance in the desperate situations that will arise between respecting sovereignty and maintaining peace and the security of mankind". The view has become increasingly accepted that the principle of nonintervention in matters that are within the domestic jurisdiction of states cannot be regarded as a protective barrier behind which human rights can be systematically violated with impunity.(8) The meeting of this challenge requires that Secondary Laws be written for the interpretation of the Articles. This will allow for clear understanding of the Primary Laws and clear Secondary Laws for their enforcement.

International Law seems to uphold the general principle of sovereignty. That is, the sanctity of territorial integrity is commonly accepted, with reservations. As outlined above, the reservations include the fact that International Law is beginning to recognize that sovereignty carries responsibilities. However, there does not appear to be succinct criteria for the abrogation of sovereignty rights. In fact, there are competing views. The lack of succinct criteria, that is, the lack of clear Secondary Laws, creates these competing views and causes much International Law to be ambiguous.

AGGRESSION

A significant issue with aggression is the ambiguity of the term. For example, Antonio Cassese,(9) makes an excellent observation: "It would be fallacious to hold the view that, since no general agreement has been reached in the world community on an exhaustive definition of aggression, perpetrators of this crime may not be prosecuted and punished". This statement makes two important points: first, it points out that perpetrators may be prosecuted;

and second it demonstrates the problem of ambiguity. If we cannot define aggression, the need for clarifying Secondary Laws becomes paramount. Without Secondary Laws how can we respond, and further, what level of response is appropriate? Cassese made this statement in his discussion of the International Military Tribunal's (IMT) attempt after World War Two to define aggression in order to assign criminal culpability to the Axis hierarchy. In the same discussion, Cassese charges that the problem with aggression was that the major Powers preferred to avoid defining this breach of the ban on force laid down in Article 2.4 of the UN Charter, so as to retain as much leeway as possible in the application of that provision both by each of them individually and by the Security Council collectively. However, it creates a problem for International Law which must deal with the ambiguity. Cassese believes the definition of aggression remains in abeyance with regard to aggression both as a state delinquency entailing international responsibility of the state and as an international crime involving criminal liability.

International institutions struggle with respect to a definition of aggression. The United Nations General Assembly adopted a deliberately incomplete definition with its resolution 3314 of December 14, 1974. The Statute of the International Criminal Court (ICC) provides for the crime of aggression but the ICC has stipulated that it will only "exercise jurisdiction" after a definition has been adopted through an amendment to its, the ICC's, charter.

The Charter of the UN treatment of aggression is seriously deficient in developing the institutions for the creation of Secondary Laws which should make interpretation clear and specific with respect to the criteria for enforcement. The issue of aggression is addressed only five times in the entire Charter and in some of those instances one must infer aggression. They are so few that they can be highlighted as follows.(10)

1. Preamble: "...that armed force shall not be used, save in the common interest..." This passage is Primary Law. It needs Secondary Law to interpret what is meant by "common interest". Does the

principle mean that armed force can only be utilized as a punishing intervention?

2. Chapter I, Article 1.1: "...suppression of acts of aggression or other breaches of the peace..." There are no Secondary Laws which interpret "acts of aggression" and what constitutes an "act of aggression" or a "breach of the peace".

3. Chapter I, Article 2.4: "All Members shall refrain in their international relations from the threat or use of force against the territorial integrity or political independence of any state..." The Secondary Law problems of this Article have been stated above. However, this Primary Law, while not naming aggression, is as close as the Charter comes to being definitive on the issue of aggression.

4. Chapter VII, Article 39: "The Security Council shall determine the existence of any threat to the peace, breach of the peace, or act of aggression..." While this author would agree that flexibility is necessary, the fact remains that there are no Secondary Laws to serve as guidelines and, therefore, the article is subject to political interpretation.

5. Chapter VIII, Article 53.1: "...renewal of aggressive policy on the part of any such state ..." "Any such state" is defined in sub-paragraph 2 of this article as any state which, during the Second World War, was an enemy of the signatories to the Charter. That provision in the Article is today a bit archaic. One could surmise that the Charter's position on aggression is that no state should initiate violence upon another state (Article 2.4) and that such acts of aggression are contrary to International Law. However, as emphasized above, the lack of defining Secondary Law and Secondary Law for enforcement against aggression often creates endless debate and, therefore, states' interpreting "aggression" as suits their national interests.

Perhaps, in an attempt to write Secondary Law to interpret aggression, the UN could borrow from Quincy Wright.(11) Writing earlier in 1935,

Wright proposed that: "A state which is under an obligation not to resort to force, which is employing force against another state, and which refuses to accept an armistice proposed in accordance with a procedure which it has accepted to implement its no-force obligation, is an aggressor, and may be subjected to preventive, deterrent remedial measures by other states bound by that obligation."

Several observations are in order with respect to Wright's characterization of aggression. Wright refers to states against states which does not address the issue of non-state actors. His use of the words "preventive" and "deterrent" could condone "preemptive" strikes.

INTERVENTION

It was noted above that in traditional common law, states could do much as they pleased including waging aggressive war. That is no longer the case. However, the common law issue of intervention is mixed. There are those who posit that any intervention is always illegal. Third World states are the foremost proponents of this view. Others believe that under certain circumstances, intervention is justified. During the 1990s, a majority of the international community came to regard military intervention to relieve human suffering and protect human rights as legitimate. In fact, military intervention often is a necessary tactic for stopping the internal conflicts that are inflicting so much human suffering.(12) The most likely proponents of this position are those who subscribe to the responsibilities of sovereignty.

There is a concept often referred to as the *Just Wars Doctrine*. The tenets of the doctrine include the principles that war is a last resort. It is directly waged to redress a wrong. It re-establishes peace. It is proportional. It does more good than harm, and of major concern for this work, it is waged under legitimate authority.(13) The Just Wars Doctrine is not a principle of International Law in part because states tend to believe that each of the belligerents may have a "just cause." However, it does take on the color of common law because its tenets are often used as a reference or justification for the use of force. In any case, the doctrine could be the basis for some Secondary Laws regarding the use of force.

In Chapter 4, "The Failure of the United Nations", we have touched on the handicaps of the Security Council with respect to intervention. We also noted the Charter's relevant articles. Now let us review the problem in greater detail. First, a brief review of the relevant Articles is in order.

Current International Law primarily vests the power of authorizing interventions with the Security Council of the UN. UN Charter Article 2.3 directs states to settle their disputes by peaceful means; Article 2.4 admonishes states not to use force or to threaten to use force in the settlement of disputes, and Article 2.7 prohibits the use of force in interventions which are essentially within the domestic jurisdiction of a given state. Article 41 of the Charter spells out the preferred methods of intervention, namely sanctions and/or the severance of diplomatic relations. Article 42 grants the Security Council the exclusive power to authorize the use of force. The only exception in the UN Charter to the prohibition of the use of force is found in Article 51 of the Charter, the right of self-defense. Even then, the party defending itself must report immediately to the Security Council and cease action as soon as the Security Council "...has taken measures necessary to maintain international peace and security...."

Quite possibly, Article 51 is the most used and abused justification for the use of force. This is the result of the fact that the Security Council is generally paralyzed in determining, 1.) what constitutes a threat to the peace and security and, 2.) what action should be taken. States will, and do, resort to Article 51. They frequently assert that their interventionist action is (was) necessitated by a threat to their national security. This exposes a weakness of the lack of interpretive Secondary Rules. If states must constantly resort to this overgeneralization, if one believes in the legality of intervention in some cases, then International Law is not setting proper guidelines for interventions.

One could take exception to the assertion that today's conflicts are not addressed by the UN Charter by citing the often used phrases in the Charter, "...[action]...to maintain or restore international peace and security..." and, as stated in Article 39, "The Security Council shall determine the existence of any threat to the peace...." While these oblique references provide flexibility, and ambiguity, they also provide a wide field for political interpretation and a license for stalemate and inaction. We must keep in mind Michael Glennon's assertion that the Security Council lacks the legal authority to interpret threats to the peace and security.(14)

This work has asserted that the lack of the specificity of Secondary Laws has led to very few UN-sanctioned interventions in the approximately 156 major conflicts since 1945.(15) In fact, there is disagreement as to what constitutes a major conflict. Richard Nixon asserted that the UN has failed to act on 170 major conflicts.(16)

It is important to note that all of the references in the Charter to the use or non-use of force are directed to state-to-state conflict. No specific Secondary Laws can be found with respect to today's typical conflicts such as terrorism, genocide, and civil conflict.

Since the 1990s, the UN has taken a greater interest in intervention in domestic and human rights issues. In the 1990s, the Security Council showed greater creativity in defining such threats.(17) Nonetheless, the fact that the Security Council finds the need to be "creative," besides the probability of being illegal, reinforces the argument that there are omissions in Secondary Laws which address these issues of aggression and intervention. Michael Glennon(18) is scathing in his assessment that there exists no coherent International Law regarding intervention. States disagree on the fundamental issues which require a consensus for laws to work. He points out that the case by case nature of decisions, or non-decisions, to intervene leave too much room for abuse. No legal remedy exists, such as a Charter amendment, because of a lack of international consensus. Therefore, we are witnessing the emergence of coalitions which weigh the costs versus the benefits of intervention.(19)

These last points highlight the three major problems associated with the lack of Secondary Laws. There is a lack of interpretive laws to eliminate ambiguity. There is a lack of enforceable Secondary Laws. Finally, there is a lack of Secondary Laws to simplify changing the laws to meet current conflict situations short of the cumbersome and possibly impossible task of Charter amendments.

Byers and Chesterman(20) go to great lengths to argue against changing the laws in International Law to render unilateral intervention legal. That is precisely the point. If Secondary Laws adequately addressed the criteria for enforcement against terrorism, genocide and human rights violations with clear Secondary Laws and Secondary Laws for timely enforcement, the issue of unilateral intervention would come up less often.

The above segues into the situation in Kosovo where NATO unilaterally, without UN approval, intervened militarily. This action has brought to the fore the issue of unilateral intervention. Jane Stromseth(21) raises the issue as to whether or not that intervention is unique or will it establish a precedent for lawful humanitarian intervention. Her view is that in the absence of Security Council will or ability, states will have to weigh humanitarian and intervention concerns against the Charter's rules governing use of force. Again, these dilemmas could be minimized if there were clearer Secondary Rules governing the interpretations of when the use of force is justified.

Because twenty-first century violence is less state-to-state conflict and more non-conventional conflict, more attention needs to be focused on the issue of preemptive strikes. Warnings of a pending aggression, such as terrorist attacks, are sometimes non-existent, obscure, elusive, or difficult to prove. Often they are known only to the security or intelligence agencies in one or more states. Sometimes the enemy is not clearly identifiable. Sometimes prior to an aggressive terrorist strike, there is no time to take the issue before the Security Council or confront the host state. Either the attack will have already occurred, or by consulting the Security Council the host state could alert the terrorist group, allowing the terrorists to melt away only to re-form at another time or place.

With the phrase "...if an armed attack occurs...", a strict interpretation of Article 51 would indicate that states may only use force after an attack. Secondary Law needs to be developed to define more clearly those circumstances in which a state may take emergency preemptive action. Richard Shultz and Andreas Vogt(22) of the Fletcher School of Law and Diplomacy, put the matter of preemptive strikes most succinctly. They posit that morally, the inclusion of preemptive operations in the concept of self-defense, or defensive intervention, is anchored in the Just War Doctrine. They also believe that the presumption in favor of self-defense is so strong that the Just War Doctrine does not confine itself exclusively to defensive measures and the legacy of the non-intervention rule. Shultz and Vogt argue that offensive operations are permitted to protect vital rights and interests unjustly "threatened", not only "injured" by other states, but also by non-state actors such as terrorist groups.

Nowhere in International Law are preemptive strikes considered legal. Therefore, states rely more heavily on an attempt at a broad interpretation of Article 51, the right of self-defense. Opponents to this tactic point to the potential of aggressive abuse. Because of that potential abuse, these opponents argue that preemptive strikes should never be allowed. On the other hand, Cassese argues that it would be naïve and self-defeating to contend that a state should wait for the attack by another state, in the full knowledge that it is certain to take place(23). He argues, "that to impose on states the attitude of sitting ducks when confronted with an impending military attack makes a mockery, both in its acceptability to states and of the Charter's main purpose of minimizing unauthorized coercion and violence across state lines".

Above, this author pointed to the need to develop International Law that allows for the rapid confrontation of an immediate problem or pending crisis.

One would hope that such a development would include Secondary Laws for controlling abuses and ensuring accountability that are the legitimate concerns of much of the world.

In summary, it is clear that the UN is effectively paralyzed by the ambiguity within International Law. That is paramount with regard to the International Law's treatment of international violence, human rights violations, genocide and other threats to the peace and security of the world. The UN should codify, simplify and reduce the volume of International Law to eliminate contradictions and ambiguity. The UN has demonstrated that it will not take on the task. If for no other reason than this, an organization such as the UGSP should take on that responsibility.

CHAPTER SIX

THE CHARTER PROVISIONS OF THE UNITED GLOBAL SECURITY PARTNERSHIP

The UN has had only limited success in the constant struggle for world peace. While a stalemate, the UN intervention into the Korean conflict prevented the destruction and domination of South Korea. In some cases UN peacekeeping forces have prevented broader problems. However, in the larger picture, sadly, it has been very difficult to arrive at the consensus necessary to take the decisive action required to prevent a small world threatening problem from becoming a major threat, conflict, or war.

Within the UN there are too many states with their own agendas. Those agendas often conflict with the settling of a problem that could have global consequences. However, the UGSP could use the UN in the humanitarian work necessary for reconstruction and to make enforcement and stabilization successful on a long term basis

NATO and SEATO may be the closest models for a UGSP. However, NATO and SEATO are basically mutual defense organizations composed of a select group of states that tend to react rather than act.

The International Court of Justice or ICJ, also known as the World Court, could be effective at administering or dispensing justice. However, as was stated in Chapter Three, the ICJ is more involved with treaty disputes between states that are willing to have the ICJ intervene.(1) Unfortunately it has no enforcement capabilities.

In the realm of violent conflict the International Criminal Court's (ICC) jurisdiction could be expanded. The UGSP could use the ICC, which does have jurisdiction over individuals accused of violence and human rights crimes, for the administering of justice in the areas where enforcement becomes necessary. The ICC has the authority to imprison convicted individuals. Currently, The ICC is hindered by the fact that the home state of the accused must agree to have its citizen tried.(2)

The UGSP could utilize its own plan to assist these organizations. The UGSP could also serve as the enforcement arm of the ICJ and the ICC. The UGSP could utilize some of the same organizational structure as NATO and SEATO in its formation. The UGSP could either assist NATO and SEATO or possibly incorporate them within the UGSP.

The world has too often witnessed the fact that the UN has been unable to prevent or solve world threatening conflicts. This is, in part, the reason the United States, Great Britain and others have had to act on their own initiative in some situations.

The UGSP would be the independent policeman of world security. It will not become involved with conflicts within an individual state's borders unless there are gross violations of international concepts of human rights, or the conflict spreads beyond those borders or there is a credible probability that it will. Should a state with a conflict within its borders request assistance from the UGSP, the UGSP could analyze the problem, take testimony from each side in the conflict, take counsel and advice from organizations such as the UN, the ICJ and/or the ICC and then decide whether an intervention is justified.

The UGSP will not be a temporary organization such as the Desert Storm (Gulf War) coalition against Iraq in 1991, but rather, it will be a permanent partnership such as NATO or SEATO. The UGSP will be constantly monitoring the world security situation.

With the end of the Cold War it was believed that there were no major military adversaries. Unfortunately, we now face threats from states such as Iran, North Korea, some African states and international terrorism. Most states recognize that violent conflicts will disrupt their economic and social growth.

When the United States was the victim of a horrific terrorist attack on September 11, 2001, the entire civilized world was shocked, angered and wanting some solutions. There could not be a more opportune time for the formation of UGSP than the first decades of the twenty-first century.

THE CHARTER

During the formation of the UGSP, great care must be taken to avoid the pitfalls of the UN. Chief among those problems are ambiguity and the lack of Primary and Secondary Laws. Therefore, the Charter of the UGSP must have clear Primary and Secondary Rules for each of the world security threats that the UGSP will address. For example, one of the Primary Rules will be, "No state shall harbor trans-state, international, terrorists". The Secondary Rules would define trans-state terrorism, the severity of trans-state terrorism that will trigger action on the part of the UGSP, and the steps of enforcement that will be employed.

International Law lawyers, statesmen and political scientists have endlessly debated the definitions and descriptions of terrorism, genocide, crimes against humanity, human rights violations, rebellions and a host of other breaches of international peace and security. There has been so much debate that the current rules and laws are so numerous, ambiguous and sometimes conflicting that states can generally interpret them as suits that state's interests. To restate, the UN has not, will not, and probably cannot simplify and codify these laws. While the task would be daunting, given the fresh start of the formation of the UGSP, clear and simple definitions and descriptions of security threats should be the cornerstones of the Charter of the UGSP.

What should be the criteria for member states of the UGSP?

The UGSP would be a global police force made up of states committed to controlling terrorism, state aggression and other threats to world peace and security. Those states must act on their own to form the organization. The UGSP cannot be formed from a group within the UN and/or sanctioned by the UN because it would be too difficult to have the UN member states agree as to which member states should be included in the UGSP. Additionally, the UN would consider it redundant to its own "peacekeeping" operations.

A love or desire for world peace is not enough. Almost all states express the desire for world peace. Unfortunately, many want world peace only after they have accomplished their individual agenda. Member states must have an unequivocal desire for world order and, along with other states, the ability and the absolute willingness to back that desire with the necessary economic and military resources to maintain world order. Member states of the UGSP shall not have territorial, political or religious ambitions beyond their borders. They can, and indeed should have, economic and social ambitions beyond their borders for the world's security. That, after all, is what we want to accomplish in this world, an interdependent world economic and social order for the secure growth of all states.

The UGSP member states must be able to recognize and be absolutely willing to eliminate a global threat, decisively, at an early stage. Member states cannot advocate a "wait and see" posture. That will only postpone the problem and its consequences and undermine the UGSP's credibility. International problems rarely cure themselves, they only become more critical.

Member states should, if possible, be a cross section of the worldwide political, geographical and religious spectrum. If that can be accomplished without diminishing the effectiveness of the UGSP then respect for UGSP authority would be established.

Which states can fulfill the criteria for membership in the UGSP?

Here in the early part of the twenty-first century the following states are examples of states that could meet the requirements:

THE UNITED STATES. The United States is the absolute most powerful state on earth, both militarily and economically. It appears to have satisfied its territorial ambitions by the early part of the twentieth century. Certainly, since the 1940's, the United States has demonstrated its desire and ability to foster world peace, and at the same time the United States has been the most generous state on earth, even to its former foes. Admittedly, the United States has taken some actions that many people deem questionable in its quest for world order. For example, during the Cold War the United States supported, contributed money to, armed, and in some cases, committed military support to repressive regimes solely because they were anti-communist.

The United States has experienced the horrific attack in September of 2001, the devastating results of terrorism. The United States has either alone, or with a "coalition", been the lead state in the fight against terrorism. The United States cannot continue or expand its current level of commitment indefinitely. The United States must have long term help from committed permanent partners.

GREAT BRITAIN. Great Britain is a good example of one state trying to control too much territory and thereby losing in the end. Essentially, the end of the "British Empire's" colonial rule occurred in the latter part of the nineteenth century. Beginning with World War Two Great Britain again became a very strong economic and military power. After World War Two Great Britain demonstrated that it no longer had territorial ambitions by the granting of independence to the last of its empire. While it is not quite that simple, it is nevertheless a fact that states such as India achieved their freedom while continuing economic and friendly ties to Great Britain. Great Britain is a democracy with a strong sense of human rights and justice and a willingness to combat terrorism. Like the United States, Great Britain has a well-organized intelligence service which can be extremely helpful in discovering problems early. Great Britain has experienced terrorism on its soil and therefore appreciates the need to stop it early.

GERMANY. In the first half of the twentieth century Germany was a good example of the need to stop an aggressive problem while it was still manageable. Since the end of World War Two, with massive aid from the wartime Allies, Germany was rebuilt into an economically powerful state with a dedication to peace and prosperity. Germany has a vast economic stake in world order and has demonstrated a willingness to help in the quest for world peace. Germany's military could be expanded to be a part of the UGSP. They too have an excellent intelligence network. Germany is not a stranger to terrorism on its soil.

JAPAN. Much of what has just been written about Germany applies also to Japan. Japan was the other major belligerent in World War Two. Like Germany, Japan was rebuilt, through Allied generosity, into a major world economic power. As a result of World War Two, Japan's military has been limited. However, it could be expanded as a partner in the UGSP. Japan still has some "fence mending" to do in Asia as a result of its actions during World War Two. Japan still has not officially acknowledged its World War Two conduct in some areas and has, therefore, not apologized in some quarters. To its credit, along with many other states that would be candidates for UGSP membership, Japan has become a generous contributor of worldwide aid. Japan's participation in the UGSP could be vital for stability in Asia. The important lessons of World War Two have not been lost on Japan. Like most of the other states on this list, Japan, too, has experienced terrorism first hand. Japan's economic stake alone would make it a valuable partner.

FRANCE. France has again become a significant economic and military power after its devastation and occupation in World War Two. Like the United States, Great Britain and others, France is a democracy and supporter of human rights and world security. Hopefully, France would see the wisdom of becoming an enthusiastic partner.

RUSSIA. After the breakup of the Soviet Union, Russia became the largest surviving state of the Soviet Union, followed by Ukraine. At the dawn of the twenty-first century Russia is still a major military power. Russia still exerts major influence in Eastern Europe and the Middle East. Russia is threatened by terrorist activity originating from states along its southern flank. In its efforts for economic recovery it has turned to the West for economic help and expanded trade. It can be hoped that Russia will eventually overcome its paranoia of a possible Western threat. Possibly, as a result of that paranoia, Russia has been attempting to regain its former power. This is exemplified by it excursion into Eastern Ukraine. Russia must begin to realize that the West is not a threat. In fact, the West has reached out to Russia in friendship and as a major trade and security partner. Therefore, Russia could be a willing partner in the UGSP. It would certainly be a vital partner. Russian intelligence, the Foreign Intelligence Service (SVR), the criminal intelligence arm (FSB) and the military intelligence (GRU) have been first rate.(3)

CHINA. Even though China has had an adversarial relationship with many of the "Free World" powers, it has been expanding its trade relations with those states. It is hopeful that the Chinese government would recognize that, like Russia, they have nothing to fear from the Western powers. It is hopeful that China would also recognize that their growing economic influence would argue very strongly for world order. China and Taiwan need to find a peaceful solution to the problem of Taiwan's relationship to China. It is in the economic interest to both to do so. Perhaps one or more states could be invited to mediate and help them come to that solution. Like Russia, China, in its western provinces, faces terrorism. China should have a great interest in being a willing, cooperative and influential partner in the UGSP.

CANADA. Canada shares the same interest and values as the United States and Great Britain. Canada also shares much of the experiences of the United States and Great Britain. Canada has shown a will and an ability to support world order.

SAUDI ARABIA. Saudi Arabia is a very wealthy and influential Middle Eastern state. If Saudi Arabia could rid itself of being a "growing field" for potential terrorist, it could be a potentially valuable partner in the UGSP. Saudi Arabia fears for its internal stability and the potential attack from neighbors. While Saudi Arabia has demonstrated a willingness to help in the fight for world stability, its fear from both within and from without have limited its help. However, with a UGSP, Saudi Arabia could be protected from external threat and, if it invited the UGSP to do so, could be helped with its internal threat. That invitation would not violate the principle that the UGSP will not become involved in the internal struggles of a state. That is because the elements that are an internal threat to Saudi Arabia are largely the same terrorist elements that are causing disruption in the entire Middle East, Southeast Asia, Southwest Asia and much of the world. Saudi Arabia could then become a major partner, a vital partner, within the UGSP.

AUSTRALIA. Strategically located off Southeast Asia, Australia, too, would be a vital partner in the UGSP. Australia has demonstrated its willingness and ability to support world order and stability. Australia has experienced terrorist attacks.

EGYPT. As of the writing of this Second Edition, Egypt has undergone a major change in government. In fact, the government of over forty years has been overthrown. It remains to be seen what policies Egypt will follow. Egypt still has its internal struggles. Like Saudi Arabia, Egypt needs to rid itself of being the witting or unwitting supplier of terrorist agents. Egypt has been reluctant to be too overt in the war on terrorism. World and certainly regional order are in its best interest. Egypt was the first state in the region to recognize the reality of Israel and attempt to help mediate solutions to the Israeli/Palestinian conflict. With help, Egypt could be a valuable and necessary partner in the UGSP.

With the current predominance of potential world destabilization being focused in the Middle East, Southwest Asia and Africa, it is extremely important that these areas be represented within the UGSP. However, in order to recruit willing and able partners many fears must be laid to rest. Through their propaganda the various terrorist networks have been successful in convincing some of the predominantly Muslim populations that the West is a great evil. It would be vital for the UGSP to assure the governments of Saudi Arabia, Egypt and others of their security in order to obtain their total willingness to aid in the removal of those terrorist networks.

As long as there exists an Israeli/Palestinian conflict, neither Israel nor a yet to-be-formed Palestinian State could be members of the UGSP. In fact, the totally objective and dedicated presence of the UGSP, along with the realization that the world has grown weary of the dangerous conflict between Israel and the Palestinians, might prompt those two adversaries to arrive at a settlement.

Other potential member states of the UGSP could include Sweden, Spain, South Korea, Brazil, Mexico, Italy, Turkey and Ukraine. One or more member-states of the African Union and its Peace and Security Council could be candidates.(4) While these states may lack the "muscle" of most of the states considered above, they could be very influential in their geographic areas. Also, some of them would need to sort their own problems. They could be helpful with intelligence and as negotiating influences with problem states.

What sort of structure should the UGSP have?

First, and most important: The number of member states must be limited to the few most capable and dedicated. That probably means no more than perhaps fifteen states. Why is that limitation important? It is important that the UGSP does not fall into the same quagmire of indecision that affects the peacekeeping duties of the UN.

Second: Each member state shall have one vote. No member state shall have a veto power which has been the "Achilles heel" for the UN Security Council. A majority vote shall rule, thus eliminating the power of the minority over the majority.

Third: All decisions as to actions of the UGSP shall be negotiated between the member states in secret. Upon agreement as to a course of action, the UGSP shall declare a consensus of the member states as to that plan of action to the world and to the offending state or group. The offending parties will be assured of the absolutely certain consequences of failure to comply with the UGSP orders. In this way there can be no doubt to the offending parties of the united, dedicated position of the UGSP.

Fourth: The UGSP may consult with other states and organizations. It may take testimony from the belligerents to arrive at a course of action. However, it will not be required to do so.

Fifth: Each of the member states shall be charged with economic and military responsibility by the charter of the UGSP. The basic criteria shall be the ability to perform. For example, it would be unrealistic to expect Canada, Mexico or Egypt to contribute as much resource as the United States. The charter-dictated proportioning of the shares of responsibility shall be strictly adhered to but with a provision for revision. That revision by majority vote would occur if a member state has had a change in economic resources or other conditions that would affect the ability to perform.

The charter should also provide for the deletion or addition of member states. It is possible that a member state may wish to voluntarily withdraw. It is also possible that the member states of the UGSP find themselves in the regrettable position of having to expel a member. There needs to be provisions within the charter to do so. There may be occasions when it is advisable to add a state to membership. There needs to be provisions for that event within the charter. In short, there needs to be provisions in the UGSP charter to allow for flexibility or change.

Sixth: Upon the identification of a problem, the UGSP shall instruct (order) the offending parties as to the actions those offending parties' shall undertake for the resolution of the problem. If it becomes necessary for the UGSP to take forceful action, that action shall be led by, with agreement of the partners, the member state with the greatest knowledge or influence in the problem area. At the very least, the state with the greatest knowledge and/or influence shall have a major role along with the chosen lead state in the execution of the UGSP's course of action. For example, it would not be wise for the United States to believe it knows more about Muslim sensitivities than Egypt or Saudi Arabia. Therefore, assuming that Saudi Arabia and Egypt are strong members in good standing in the UGSP, they should have leading roles, either militarily or as highly visible advisors, in any action undertaken by the UGSP in the Middle East, Southeast Asia and Southwest Asia. The lack of understanding of the culture has been a major contributing cause for the continued unresolved conflict in both Iraq and Afghanistan.

Seventh: Given an understanding of the cultural norms of the subject state, all decisions of the UGSP shall be "blind" to the political, religious, economic and social interest of the belligerents or the member states of the UGSP. This will lead to more just decisions of the UGSP and vastly increase the credibility of the UGSP in the court of world opinion. Being "blind" means that while understanding the cultural norms of a state those cultural norms shall not influence UGSP actions. The UGSP's sole mission shall be the maintenance of world order and world peace. It will accomplish that mission by the termination of a potentially global threatening situation in its early stages, while it is still manageable. If necessary, the UGSP will terminate the threat with military action or the credible warning of military action. If the UGSP is strong enough, dedicated enough and its actions are focused, sure and decisive, it might not require too many military actions before the mere warning of such action will dissuade would-be opportunists from attempts at destabilizing the world order.

By being "blind" to the political, religious, economic and social interest of an area in conflict, the actions of the UGSP cannot be criticized as being opportunistic in the world court of public opinion.

Let us make no mistake, what is being proposed is a no nonsense global police force. This is an idea that is not particularly popular. Many states will view the formation of the UGSP as a threat to their sovereignty. Interestingly, many of those who will object are the very reason for the necessity.

CHAPTER SEVEN

THE OPERATIONAL PLAN OF THE UNITED GLOBAL SECURITY PARTNERSHIP

The first part of the title of this work is *A Measured Response*, therefore what follows are the EIGHT basic principles of the UGSP plan for the execution of the UGSP orders which constitute that *Measured Response*.

How, then does the UGSP initiate action?

ONE: THE UNITED GLOBAL SECURITY PARTNERSHIP CONDUCTS AN INVESTIGATION, INITIATES A PLAN OF ACTION.

When a problem has been identified by the UGSP, the member states will begin an investigation. The information and the views of each member shall be secret. The UGSP may, but is not obliged to, seek testimony from the offending governments and groups, surrounding states, the UN, individual or group experts on the problem, etc. After the secret deliberations of the member states has culminated in a secret majority vote, a consensus and a united decision shall be announced to the offending parties and to the world. That announcement shall take the form of a report to the offending parties and to the world as to the facts in the case and the justification for the UGSP's interest in the matter. It will further detail in unmistakable terms, exactly the course of action the offending parties are ordered to take. It will also, in clear and decisive terms, outline the certain action of the UGSP if the offending parties do not obey the order.

Throughout this text when reference is made to "terrorist cell", the terrorist cells are being used as examples. One could substitute, and this work is certainly referring to any individual, group or state with ambitions that could threaten world order and stability.

Before this discussion can go any further, it must be established which kinds of issues will trigger a UGSP response and which kinds of issues shall be of no interest to the UGSP. In other words, it is important to identify world threatening problems as opposed to those problems which are strictly internal. With the exception of genocide or gross violations of human rights, for those problems that are strictly internal the UGSP should not interfere with the sovereignty of that state. The following are theoretical examples:

1. Within the borders of a state, an individual, a group or a political party is attempting to overthrow the existing government. They are using violence as well as propaganda in their attempt. It matters not the type of political practices the existing government employs, this is strictly a domestic problem outside the purview of the UGSP unless genocide or the gross violation of human rights is involved. If, however, the threatening group is headquartered or has bases of operation in a foreign state, the UGSP shall warn or take action against the state that is hosting that group.

   Regardless of how abhorrent the targeted government which is being attacked by the rebellious group, the UGSP shall not interfere if the violence is within their borders. The UGSP shall, in this situation, become involved when and if the issue becomes international.

2. When a rebellious group is attempting to arouse public support solely within their own state (state A) by using rhetoric and propaganda against an outside state (state B) or group of states (B, C and D), the UGSP shall have an interest. For example, the rebellious group cites their own government's (state A) alleged support for the policies of an outside government (states B, C and/or D), which, according to the rebellious group's propaganda, is injuring the population of state A. Further, the rebellious group is promising the population that, when they come to power within state A, they will deal with that outside government (states B, C and/or D) and its policies. This now becomes a possible threat to future world peace and stability. Again, it does not matter whether or not the UGSP and/or its member states agree with the actions and policies of the government that was targeted by the rebellious group. The rebellious group, in this case, is the possible disrupting problem. That group must be dealt with and, the UGSP has a legitimate interest. However, if the rebellious group in state A is limiting itself to peaceful rhetoric against their own state because of its support of state B and state B is, in fact, a real threat, the UGSP will have an interest in the activities of state B. The UGSP must recognize that, for legitimate reasons, the citizens of a state have the right to replace by peaceful means, but with violence if necessary, their state's government.

3. There is no acceptable reason for any state to develop or increase their inventory of nuclear, biological and/or chemical weapons. These are not viable defensive weapons. A government manufacturing such weapons can only have offensive objectives in mind. This author recognizes that many of the states listed as members of the UGSP have stockpiles of nuclear, chemical and biological weapons. States such as the United States, Russia, China, etc. must take the lead and destroy or vastly reduce their stockpiles. Along with nuclear

weapons being reduced, the elimination of biological and chemical weapons among the member states of the UGSP can be achieved by negotiations and trust building between the member states. With confidence in their mutual alliance, collective strength and resolve and because of the example they have set, the UGSP can then demand that other states such as Iran, North Korea, India, Pakistan, etc. do the same. Clearly, this is an area in which the UGSP has an interest. In the case of Iran, the existing government has been making a concerted effort to develop its nuclear capability. Iran has demonstrated its hostile intent with its support of terrorism and its antagonism against Israel and the West. The same situation applies to North Korea. Solve a problem while it is still manageable. As of this writing, during the first half of 2015 four Western powers (the U. S., Great Britain, France and Germany) plus Russia and China have tried to negotiate a ban on Iran's work toward a nuclear weapon. Iran has rejected any inspection provisions of any agreement. Most of the world has little confidence that Iran would live up to an agreement or give up terrorist sponsorship. The situation is not going to get better, only worse. To think otherwise is wishful thinking. The UGSP would have a compelling reason to interfere with Iran now!

4. The UGSP would have a legitimate reason to order two warring states to "cease fire" and "stand down". Those two states would be ordered to take their grievances to an arbitrating third party, the UN, ICC or the ICJ. The UGSP would then have a right to insure that the edicts of that third party settlement are enacted. Indeed, the UGSP would have the right to enforce those edicts.

5. A terrorist group with a particular ideology may conduct a raid upon a state or a group of states. It is apparent that their base of operations or the origination of the attack came from another state or group of states. The UGSP in this case will have a right to order

those states of origination to search out and destroy the terrorist groups. Failure to do so will cause intervention by the UGSP in the affairs of the originating state or states. For example, in the early part of the twenty-first century, Pakistan has been a relatively safe haven for both al Qaeda and the Taliban.

6. If a state invites the UGSP to help them with an internal problem the UGSP may consider doing so. This does not mean that a government can utilize the UGSP to put down an internal threat to that government's power. In other words, the UGSP will not allow itself to be a convenient extension of that government's army. Rather, it means that with the consensus of the UGSP's member states, helping the inviting government would further world stability. A good example would be helping, if invited, states such as Saudi Arabia and Yemen in their struggles with terrorist organizations such as al Qaeda. The UGSP could first help with intelligence support and then, if necessary and invited, military support. That support would be designed to rout out and destroy terrorist groups which are a threat to the stability of those governments. In Saudi Arabia and Yemen it would appear that terrorist cells are reaching out worldwide. The UGSP would, under the criteria outlined above, have an interest even if uninvited. However, Saudi Arabia has expressed a desire to be rid of the terrorist cells. It only remains to be seen if they are capable of doing so on their own.

In the formulation of a plan of action, "a measured response", all of the above must be taken into consideration. All possible scenarios and their consequences must be explored. Because every situation is different, it is impossible to forecast all of the possible problems or consequences, nonetheless an exhaustive investigation will likely avoid major unwanted surprises.

TWO: ANY GOVERNMENT UNABLE OR UNWILLING TO TERMINATE THEIR AGGRESSIVE ACTIONS AGAINST ANOTHER STATE OR ELIMINATE THEIR TERRORIST CELLS SHALL BE GIVEN THE OPPORTUNITY TO IMMEDIATELY SURRENDER THEIR ARMED FORCES TO THE UNITED GLOBAL SECURITY PARTNERSHIP.

It should be made clear that not all states with terrorist cells will require even the orders outlined in "Section One" above. There are many states which realize that they have been unwittingly harboring and/or been the "growing field" for such cells. Some of those states have both the willingness and the ability to solve the problem within their borders. For example, after the September, 2001 attack upon the United States, the United States realized that through its lapses in intelligence, there appeared to be a growing number of terrorist cells working in secret within the borders of the United States. The United States initiated a massive investigation utilizing all the facilities of its Federal Bureau of Investigation (FBI), the Central Intelligence Agency (CIA) and other intelligence gathering groups within the U. S. federal government. The United States has utilized the intelligence gathering and law enforcement capabilities of numerous other governments. This activity has resulted in hundreds of arrests worldwide and the effort is ongoing. Similar actions are taking place in Great Britain, Germany, Spain, France and several other states.

Some states, wittingly or unwittingly, have harbored terrorist cells. While some of those states are willing to eliminate the cells within their borders, some are unable to do so for lack of law enforcement, inadequate military or political reasons. For example, Saudi Arabia is a "growing field" for terrorist fighters. The propaganda machinery of the terrorist has made it a holy cause to rid the world, in the name of Islam, of the infidels, Zionists and the "crusading" evil West. They have been successful in selling this line to vast numbers of people in Saudi Arabia and the rest of the Arab world.

Curiously, some of these terrorist cells are reportedly supported by wealthy and influential Saudi families and businesses. The Saudi government fears that an overt crackdown on these terrorist cells and their supporters could, through a popular uprising, threaten the stability of the Saudi government. Even though the Saudi government has been somewhat duplicitous in its approach to the problem, they seem to have a real interest in solving the unrest, armed conflicts, and the great threat to Middle East and Southeast Asia security and stability. Therefore, before the UGSP would issue orders in examples like this, and there are many, the "good offices" of the UGSP should be offered. The UGSP could meet, in secret if necessary, with those governments and outline a plan that would eliminate the terrorist cells yet be "comfortable" to the government in question.

Diplomacy is often indecisive. With the above idea, reference is not being made to an indecisive approach. Rather, through diplomacy, the concept outlined in the above paragraph establishes a plan that, with its execution by the willing government in question, will accomplish the goal of ridding the state of its terrorist cells. In these cases the UGSP is offering the problem state intelligence gathering help, public assistance and education to change the thinking of the population and, if necessary, arms, military help and possibly "surgical" strikes. It would only be after a failure of the agreed upon plan and the discontinuance of the co-operation of the problem government that the UGSP would exert its full authority.

In the case of a problem state that is just not willing to co-operate, or is belligerent, they might first be given the opportunity to see the errors of their ways and the absolute consequences. If, because of the decisiveness of the UGSP, the unwilling problem-government realizes that it is very much in their best interest to become a willing-government, then the above discussion would apply. If, however, they have other motives or are still not willing to co-operate with the world in the elimination of violence and terrorism, then the UGSP would commence one or more of sections "Three" through "Eight", which follows.

The UGSP would then direct the problem state, or states, to immediately adhere to the orders of the UGSP. The problem state would be directed to cease their aggressive action or locate and eliminate the aggressors or terrorists cells within their state, leaving no doubt as to the consequences of failure. Their willingness to do so will determine whether or not the UGSP will allow that government to remain in power.

At this point, the UGSP would, after its investigation, announce its clear course of action to the problem government and the world. That course of action would include inviting the problem government to co-operate. One of the first steps in that co-operation would be the placing of that nation's police forces and military under the control of a UGSP command. It is important to impress upon the leadership of the government, the police forces and the military of the certain consequences of their failure to co-operate. This is particularly true if the problem is governmental aggression. It is important to give the problem government a clear incentive to co-operate or step aside. That incentive may mean the ability to stay alive, limited incarceration or, as repugnant as it may seem, the ability to retire in comfortable exile.

The resultant elimination of command and control is vitally important to minimizing armed resistance. Very often, a leaderless army is easy to subdue and control. Such an event could give the UGSP the opportunity to occupy the problem state before the military and/or the police forces have the ability to find new leadership and regroup.

THREE: IF UNITED GLOBAL SECURITY PARTNERSHIP INTERVENTION IS REQUIRED, THE INITIAL MILITARY ACTION MUST BE PRECISE.

Before any overt military action is taken the careful plan of action shall be developed. It should be obvious that every situation is different. Some terrorist cells are easily identified as to the principals and their locations.

Others are not so easily identified. If it is a vocal and/or violent political organization such as the Nazis in the 1920's and the 1930's, they may be fairly easy to target. Geographic conditions will differ. Some problems may be localized in strictly urbanized areas. Some will be in deserts, mountains, jungle or a combination of terrains and rural or urban settings. In some of these cases, immediate military action may not be prudent. It is possible that counter-intelligence, propaganda, infiltration, surgical strikes or even, select assassination may correct the problem.

In the case of state sponsored aggression a careful assessment of what form of military action, the amount of force, the governmental targets and locations must be made. This is particularly important in order to minimize civilian casualties. Knowledge of the culture is vital so as to minimize any citizen resentment.

The point in this discussion so far is that a careful plan, "a measured response" must be designed to fit the exact situation that the UGSP is confronting. Therefore, let us recap.

After the plan has been developed, without disclosing logistic and strategic secrets, the belligerents and the world should be told exactly what is going to happen. That disclosure will leave no doubt that the announced plan is, in fact, exactly what will happen. There are at least three advantages to that tact:

First: The plan may give the belligerents an opportunity to reconsider their position and its consequences.

Second: The plan will tell the world what is happening so that there are no shocks.

Third: The plan could give civilians an opportunity to get out of harm's way.

Explaining the plan to the belligerents and the world and making clear the consequences of failure to comply could trigger a popular uprising against the belligerents. Granted, it could cause a popular uprising against the UGSP. However, if that is the case, that uprising might have happened anyway, and in this instance, the UGSP would be forewarned that they are going to have a civilian problem.

By planning and executing a step by step action there are at least four advantages which can be obtained:

1. It gives the belligerents many opportunities to reconsider and surrender with a minimal loss of life.
2. It can minimize political damage. There will be a discussion below regarding the seeds of future conflicts.
3. It can greatly reduce the cost in lives and materiel by the precise targeting of strategic military targets and installations.
4. By surgically eliminating strategic military targets and installations, usually through airpower, the UGSP can reduce the belligerent's will and ability to fight with a minimum of risk to the UGSP forces.

The philosophy and military tactic outlined in "Three" and "Four" above, was well learned with a great deal of success by the United States led coalition against Iraq in the "Desert Storm" action in 1991. That action successfully terminated Iraq's invasion and occupation of Kuwait. Although, in many cases the use of air power and "surgical strikes" alone may not be sufficient. It may be necessary for "boots on the ground".

A discussion of the Iraq/Kuwait "Desert Storm" action is a casebook study of how a UGSP action should or could be executed. During the building of the coalition by the United States against Iraq, Iraq was given plenty of opportunity to reverse its course, and Iraq and the world was well informed as to what the outcome was going to be. Unwisely, Iraq choose not to do so. A good part of that decision may have been doubt on the part of the Iraqi leadership as to the commitment of the United States. Iraq may have doubted the ability of the United States to gain sufficient support for the coalition. That Iraqi viewpoint was helped by the weak diplomatic maneuvering of the United Nations. Nevertheless, sufficient warning was given.

When it became necessary for the military operation to begin it was well executed. Through the use of very high tech, sophisticated airborne weapons, Iraqi command and control facilities were destroyed and the Iraqi Air Force gutted. Iraq flew some military aircraft to Iran, their arch enemy, for safety. Their artillery and troop strength was greatly diminished. With the skies secure, extensive coalition bombing of military troops and their installations exhausted the Iraqi military. Coalition ground troops found very little opposition upon occupation and clean-up with very few coalition casualties. There was a minimum of civilian casualties because of the careful planning and execution. Additionally, but very important, except for occasional orchestrated rallies, there was very little adverse political fallout from the "Desert Storm" operation.

FOUR: UTILIZING THE COMBINED INTELLIGENCE GATHERING CAPABILITIES OF THE UNITED GLOBAL SECURITY PARTNERSHIP MEMBER STATES, SPECIAL TEAMS SHALL ELIMINATE THE TERRORIST CELLS OR "ROGUE" STATE LEADERS

Before any action is taken the intelligence must be first rate and reliable. Many of the states proposed as member states of the UGSP have excellent intelligence operations. Given the proposed diversity of states within the UGSP and their diverse perspectives and resources, the resultant intelligence will be far better than any individual state could gather on its own. Additionally, depending on the nature of a particular problem, some non-member states may very likely be willing to contribute intelligence. This will be especially true if they have been convinced that it is very much in their national interest to co-operate.

Building on the premise of "Section Three" above that the initial military action must be precise, some of the actions in this discussion may be executed in tandem with or even before such actions as "surgical" air strikes.

The key is that the initial enforcement of the edicts of the UGSP must be ruthless and efficient. Most terrorist and most ambitious "rogues" have no rules except to do whatever is necessary to accomplish their ends. Therefore, the UGSP's enforcement must take whatever actions are necessary to inflict the greatest possible unnerving damage to the target group, without any limitations. Those are the terrorist's rules of engagement and so they must be the UGSP's rules of engagement. However, the UGSP shall not employ the use of barbaric torture tactics that appear to be popular with some terrorist organizations. The enforcement must also be efficient. That is, if actions can be planned and executed so as to minimize the large scale involvement of UGSP assets and exposure, and those actions can minimize civilian exposure, they should be utilized. In any case, early enforcements by the UGSP should be so devastating and demoralizing to the targeted groups so as to discourage future world security threatening ambitions.

Let us address the "problem" of assassination. If it is warranted it should not be a problem. We must keep in mind that we are dealing with a world security threatening individual or group. These are individuals or groups that if given the opportunity, would create havoc with an unknown number of casualties. If it can be ascertained that the assassination of one or more of the leaders of the target group will cause the dissolution of that group and solve the problem, then that (those) assassination(s) must occur. There should be no "moralizing". It must be decisive. It is doubtful that, given the chance, the target group would pass an opportunity to assassinate. This is a consideration for an early preventative move and a possible early solution. It could save many more lives than it cost. The world and the offender would have been advised beforehand of the UGSP plan of action.

This author is not advocating the wholesale employment of assassination. Before such an action is undertaken the intelligence must be exact. It must be clear that the probability of success is nearly perfect. A failure could be disastrous from the standpoints of politics, propaganda and morale. It must be clear that the success will vastly advance the solution of the problem. It must be clear that it will minimize current and future casualties. Future outcomes of the action must be clearly considered including future political consequences. The question of possibly greater future problems as a result of the assassination(s) must be considered. For example, in the case of "rogue" government leaders, are there replacement leaders standing in the wings so that a void is not created? Additionally, is the targeted individual or individuals highly revered and would their assassination cause a significant popular backlash?

What follows is a look at some possible scenarios for the above discussion:

1. Collective intelligence has determined that the leader of the target group is, in fact, a very strong leader. That leader is the driving force of the group, and his removal would cause the group to disintegrate. Further, intelligence has identified a behavior pattern and pinpointed a frequented location with little risk of collateral damage. It has been determined that the elimination of the leader of the target group would not cause political damage beyond the group. This is definitely a candidate for an assassination.

2. If it is determined that the leader of the target group is a charismatic, potential leader of a broad based population, such as a religious group, it may be far more prudent to deal with that leader later as the solution to the problem unfolds. Obviously, if any of the criteria for approving an assassination cannot be satisfactorily met, assassination is out of the question. If, for example, it is determined that the second or third in command in the target group would be a greater threat, then the leader should be left in place. When the final solution of the problem has been achieved the fate of that leader and his associates can be determined.

Careful consideration must be given to the long term political consequences of the immediate liquidation or removal of the leadership. It must be weighed against the magnitude of current and future casualties. To prevent possible political, propaganda or morale damage, success must be nearly assured. If these criteria can be met, either special teams or individuals would complete the mission. If they cannot be met, save dealing with the leadership until a more opportune time, or capture them during or at the conclusion of the operation. It is often the case that a leaderless group will dissolve or be much more easily captured or controlled.

In this work it has been stressed that the enforcement should be no-nonsense, ruthless and efficient in order to discourage future individuals or groups from threatening world peace. If, at the conclusion of a UGSP enforcement action, the UGSP finds itself with prisoners from the target group, including leaders, those prisoners should be dealt with in a fashion that is not in the public view. This does not mean in total secret but with limited public knowledge (publicity) until the end results have been decided. This does not mean that the individuals will be deprived of reasonable justice and representation. What it does mean is that by limiting publicity, the ability to become "martyrs" or political or religious heroes during the trials will be diminished.

It will likely be determined that some of the prisoners were merely "foot soldiers" with no additional threat and shall therefore be freed. Some will have varying degrees of culpability and will require appropriate prison time. Some of the leadership may warrant a death sentence. If their threat to world order is so great and/or the consequences of their misadventure has created considerable damage, there should be no question as to the justification of the death penalty. For the administration and dispensing of justice the UGSP will utilize the ICC.

3. There will be situations in which none of the above actions have solved the problem and it will be necessary to employ a large armed force to eliminate the problem, restore order and restructure and rebuild the problem state. This does not mean that the UGSP will suddenly place thousands of UGSP troops on the ground, although in some situations that action may be prudent. A "large armed force" may mean stepped up air power. It may mean the employment of native troops with UGSP training, assistance and guidance. This event very much emphasizes the importance of the

permanency of the UGSP and the importance of the diversity of its member states.

It is vitally important that in the UGSP secret planning sessions, the UGSP recognizes and plans for the possibility of a large scale military action and a possible occupation of the targeted state. The resultant plan must then be announced to the target state and to the world in order to minimize political surprise and possible world criticism.

A large scale military action should not be undertaken prematurely. The military and the economic power of the UGSP will very likely be far superior to any target group or state. However, where possible, the UGSP should employ local groups that share the UGSP goals for their state. Those groups could spare the UGSP costly mistakes. The UGSP must recognize that if a large scale military action and occupation will be necessary, the above discussed measures should be taken along with the economic and logistic starvation of the targeted regime. This means the reduction or elimination of the targeted state's ability to fight. That will happen through air power and "commando" operations targeting aircraft, artillery, naval, supply (ammunition and fuel), troop concentrations, command and control. It will also involve choking off the money supply line and, if possible, the sealing of the borders to prevent re-supply. Given these actions, time will be on the side of the UGSP.

When accurate intelligence has determined that the targeted state is sufficiently weakened to allow for the "relatively safe" invasion by UGSP forces, that force should be of such a size as to further demoralize the opposition and cause a rapid conclusion to the hostilities. That force should be so overwhelming as to minimize actual combative resistance and thereby minimize both civilian and military casualties. Unfortunately, in too many cases, it has been "force as necessary". That tactic would rob the UGSP of the initiative and prolong the fighting and casualties. It bears repeating: The force must be crushing.

FIVE: THE UNITED GLOBAL SECURITY PARTNERSHIP
SHALL OCCUPY AND ADMINISTER THE PROBLEM STATE
UNTIL THE REMOVAL OF THE WORLD THREAT HAS BEEN
ACHIEVED AND STABILIZATION HAS BEEN RESTORED.
IN SOME CASES THIS COULD BE YEARS OR EVEN A
GENERATION OR MORE.

This "Section Five", "Six", "Seven" and "Eight" to follow are so closely tied and related that they will tend, in many cases, to run together. This section refers to martial law. Upon the occupation of the problem state and at the cessation of hostilities, ironclad control must be initiated until the situation can be assessed and relative stabilization has occurred.

In some situations, even though open hostilities have ended and the leaders of the world threat have been removed, there could well be pockets of resentment and potential hostilities. If those pockets are ignored, new leadership could occur and the problem could flare again. Once again, excellent intelligence is vital. Vigilance is definitely required. Redevelopment of the problem must not be tolerated. It must be immediately dealt with in such a way as to completely discourage its continuation. This may seem dictatorial and oppressive. It is. However, one cannot go about winning the hearts and minds of the population or rebuilding the state if one must continually put out "brushfires". Ignored brushfires become forest fires. Solve the problem while it is still manageable.

It was discussed earlier in this work, but bears repeating, that one must keep in mind that many of the world security threatening conflicts have had their seeds planted many years, generations or even centuries before the threat escalated to the point where it would be necessary for the UGSP to take action. Therefore, in some cases, there are generations such as grandfathers, fathers and children that harbor deep resentments and wounds. It does not matter whether or not those resentments and wounds are justified. They must be dealt with in the rebuilding. However, they must also be unconditionally controlled or stabilization will not occur and nothing will have been accomplished.

In some cases in the past a "quick fix" has been the order of the day. The targeted state has been left to its own inadequate capabilities and, not surprisingly, the old problem or worse has resurfaced. That situation has also led to the deeper resentments for the state or states that intervened in the first place. It follows that those resentments have hampered the ability to organize other subsequent peacekeeping coalitions.

In some cases strong martial law will, of necessity, have been part of the UGSP's plan. That plan will have been explained in advance to the offending state and to the world so that there are no surprises and therefore, minimal world criticism. Sadly, but conveniently, because the UGSP will very likely be replacing an oppressive regime, the population will very probably be accustomed to martial law.

The imposition of martial law does not mean the ironclad control of people's daily lives or the invasion of their privacy or human rights. It means the monitoring and control of the state's police and military and the elimination of any remaining hostile individuals or groups. As control is gained and stabilization is improved, martial law can be gradually relaxed.

The stability and control is necessary not only to prevent the reoccurrence of the problem, but to allow for the rebuilding of the state. Administrators, aid workers, medical teams and educators must be able to operate in a peaceful, stable environment in order to be effective. The population must be assured of peace and security in order to be receptive of the rebuilding process. As stated above, the martial law will not invade the private lives of the general population. Quite the contrary, martial law will insure that no group invades the private lives or endangers the security and safety of the population. Martial law will thereby reassure the population as to the motives of the UGSP. This could greatly facilitate the ability of the UGSP to rebuild the state with the support of the population.

This work has emphasized that the primary goal of the UGSP is the maintenance of global security and that the achievement of that goal is very possibly through enforcement and police actions. Now, in this section and the sections which follow, Sections Six through Eight, this work will address occupation, rebuilding and transitions within the offending state. While these activities are a vital part of the overall solution they run the risk of overwhelming the resources of the UGSP. Further, there are other organizations with potentially greater resources that could assist at this point. That must be encouraged. However, the UGSP must maintain an overview position with the ability to quickly intervene if the stated solution is not being achieved or there is a serious deviation from the plan to achieve the stated solution.

For example, upon initial occupation, it may be determined that the humanitarian resources of the UN would be highly desirable or, in fact, necessary. The UN is far better suited to fill that role than the UGSP. However, as has sometimes been demonstrated in the past, the UN would probably not be as effective in immediately controlling or preventing the reoccurrence of hostilities or agitation. The UN would probably be better suited in aiding the establishment and supervision a new government. However, as has been stated, overall control would remain with the UGSP until such a time as true security has been demonstrated.

After the planned and announced decisive acquisition of control and the no-nonsense continuation of control, future ambitious regimes may very well carefully reconsider their adventures. As the UGSP unconditionally exerts authority through carefully announced and precisely executed plans for enforcing world stability, more people will become believers. That could translate into a situation where, if through its stated actions, the UGSP has demonstrated that it will absolutely enforce world stability, its need to do so could diminish. In other words, ambitious "rogues", groups or states may come to recognize that their actions will be thwarted, that they will not succeed and that they will be punished. In the world at the beginning of the twenty-first century there exists no such organization that engenders that kind of realization, not the United States, the "Western Allies", NATO or the UN.

SIX: THE UNITED GLOBAL SECURITY PARTNERSHIP SHALL DETERMINE THE FORM OF GOVERNMENT EACH OCCUPIED STATE SHALL HAVE DURING OCCUPATION. HUMAN RIGHTS WILL BE RESTORED AND GUARANTEED. THE POPULATION SHALL BE MADE SECURE.

In the previous section, it was stated that the UGSP shall "occupy and administer" the problem state. This section will address the events and policies after the initial occupation.

In some cases, in part depending upon the degree of co-operation from the existing government of the problem state, it may be determined that the existing government does not need replacing. It may be that some people need to be removed, and that a period of supervision may be necessary, but the existing government can be preserved. When this occurs the UGSP will take the initial steps necessary to restart a functioning existing government. The UGSP may decide to use its own resources to supervise that government until security has been clearly demonstrated and another entity, such as the UN, can take control.

If the UGSP has had to intervene militarily and occupy, the old government may need to be dismantled and replaced. It will be within the jurisdiction of the UGSP to do just that. As stated in the last section it might be wiser to bring in help from other world organizations such as the UN. However, the UGSP does not relinquish control.

In the West we believe that a democratic form of government which encourages free enterprise, free speech, freedom of religion and with all the other personal freedoms those governments afford, is the best form of government known. Governments and the states that embrace these democratic principals have been extremely successful. Therefore, we believe all states should have that form of government, and we have pressured states to take that path. Unfortunately, that is not what is best for every state. Many societies are just not ready or capable and for others it is not desirable.

There are states in which a democratically based government could be established after the world security-threatening situation has been resolved. Typically these would be states in which there has been some degree of democracy in the past so that the population has had some experience with the concept. It is important to note that "having the vote" does not a democracy make. It is a rare dictator that does not give the population, or an influential portion of the population, the right to vote. Those governments however, control the election.

States which have a high rate of literacy and advanced education are states that could be moved toward a democratic society. So, too could states with a significant degree of free enterprise and personal freedoms. If the state has had experience with freedom of the press and religion, along with literacy, they too, are candidates. It is, of course, interesting to note that states that have high literacy, free enterprise, an uncontrolled vote, freedom of the press and religion are rarely problem states with world threatening leaders or groups.

Some states are capable of being democracies, others need authoritarian rule. Many states that will need UGSP intervention are not ready to be democracies. To try to force democracy upon them could be disastrous. It is a sad analogy but a true analogy that you cannot give an infant or small child total freedom of choice. They require years of education, experience and maturity before they are capable of making their own decisions. The same is true, though we are loathe to express it, of societies. A poor, semi-literate "third world" state may need a "benevolent dictator" guiding it until the population has achieved literacy and has gained experience in the concepts of democracy before it can become a democracy. Being that guiding "benevolent dictator" will be the job of the UGSP and/or its designee. Hopefully democracy, but definitely stability, will be the long-term goal.

While it is relatively easy for a rogue group to foment world threatening dissention among "poor, semi-literate third world" populations, far more advanced states can be problem states. However, a common thread runs throughout. That thread is oppression. That oppression is usually at the hands of the existing government. That government, if it is opportunistic, will exploit that oppression by blaming another entity against which the state must crusade. A rogue individual or group will also exploit oppression with the intent of carrying the crusade beyond the borders. Even if that state has had some experience with democracy, once the UGSP has had to intervene and occupy, attempting to bring that state back to an immediate democracy could be a mistake. It is very likely that much foundation work must first be done. The work necessary to bring a society to the point of being an educated democracy will be discussed below and more completely outlined in Section Eight.

The UGSP, or its designee, must determine the needs of the occupied state. Among other considerations, they should assess literacy, health, infrastructure and the economic conditions within the occupied state. They must develop an understanding of the degree of sophistication and experience in government within the occupied state. They must then develop the plan for a government that will provide long-term stability and security. It may well be that the government will initially be a totalitarian government. The plan must clearly outline the steps that will be employed to move that government along the path to a free society.

It may take years or even generations to remove the old animosities and for the population to gain the necessary experience to move the form of government, step by step, to a democratic government. It may very well be that a pure democracy will not be the end goal of the UGSP. If, by the standards of a given society, the people have an acceptable level of personal freedom, that society may function very well and be happy with a monarchy. It may be a monarchy or a government based upon and ruled by religious principles.

It was stated earlier that in many cases the population will have been subjected to totalitarian rule by the prior government. Therefore the initial imposition of a controlled government will not be unusual to that society. That is a sad but convenient situation. In fact, many within the population will just resign themselves to yet another dictatorial government. Given that, there is a real danger that elements of the group that caused the initial need for intervention will attempt to rally support. There is the real danger that they could have some success. The UGSP must quell that possibility. Besides thwarting those groups it will be the job of the UGSP to incorporate within their redevelopment plan great emphasis on the personal welfare of the population. It will do no good to publicize great goals of personal freedom, etc. to a population that only has a vague understanding of those concepts.

The redevelopment plan must include human rights and personal security. The implementation of human rights and personal security will go a long way towards winning the hearts and minds of the population. It must also be remembered that the seeds of future problems are sown by the way an action is prosecuted today.

At the very outset, even before the campaign for most human rights, the sense of personal safety and security must be impressed upon the population. They must know and be confident of the fact that they will be safe in their homes, job place and on the streets. They must know that they have no fear of attack by government, military, police or any group. They must know they have no fear of summary arrest. Freedom of religion must be guaranteed from the outset. The freedom to pursue free enterprise must be encouraged even where free enterprise has not been experienced. The population must be able to believe and must be able to rely upon those assurances. The establishment of the other basic human rights with the UGSP regulated government insuring that those rights are honored must be put in place. They must know that the sins of the previous regime are no more. While it may seem a paradox, this is part of the reason why the initial government, controlled by the UGSP, will probably need to be dictatorial. That government will have to insure against those who would threaten the population.

As with the post Soviet era Russia, the immediate institution of free enterprise, across the board, may be difficult or impossible. There is the danger, as happened in Russia, that elements of the prior regime may attempt to exploit state assets that rightfully need to be redistributed in a fair and equitable manner. The UGSP must guard against that possibility. In all likelihood, only those who understand free enterprise will participate initially. Others will follow along.

The right to an education, which will be discussed in Section Eight, must be established. In the early stages the right to assembly and the free press may have to be monitored or restricted. As the last remnant of the problem group is eliminated, the rights to assembly and the free press can be expanded. Most assuredly, if there is complete freedom of assembly and a total free press while there are still pockets of the problem group, they will use those opportunities to create mischief.

It is worth restating at this point that these actions will go a long way toward winning the hearts and minds of the population and validating the credibility of the UGSP in the eyes of the world. Moving a problem state's government to self-rule or home rule will go a long way toward accomplishing those positive goals.

SEVEN: THE UNITED GLOBAL SECURITY PARTNERSHIP GOAL SHALL BE THE RETURN OF SELF-RULE BY THE UTILIZATION OF LOCAL ADMINISTRATORS AND THE DEVELOPMENT OF FUTURE LEADERS.

It is possible that as stability increases within the UGSP occupied state the presence of the UGSP's military power should decrease. As progress continues the UGSP and the UN should be identifying individuals and organizations within the occupied state that are capable of taking on increasing amounts of responsibility.

There will be a discussion in greater detail in Section Eight as to the needs for education for the general population. Here, we want to concern ourselves with the educational skills necessary for the population to understand government and for certain members of the population to gain the skills necessary to help administer the government.

Historically, the attempts by an occupying state to attempt "nation building" within the occupied state have not worked well in all cases. A possible reason for those failures may be the attempts to rebuild the occupied state in the image of the occupying state. This work has stressed that "nation building" must adhere to the occupied state's customs, social norms, religion and the form of government that is most preferred by the population of the occupied state. This principle must hold even if those societal norms are abhorrent to the UGSP.

For the general population, literacy is the first issue. If the population can read and comprehend what they have read and the occupying government is forthcoming with information as to progress and goals, the population will feel more connected to the government. The population will also be more receptive to local "native" administrators and officials. It will be easier to dispel the notion that those local officials are just mere "puppets" of the UGSP's occupying government. Further, if the government is forthcoming with information to a literate society, it will be easier to recruit quality candidates from the population for administrative positions.

A careful analysis of the state's history must be made. It may well be that the state is better suited to a monarchy, if that is their history, or a religion based government. The population must be educated as to that political history and they must be educated as to the other governmental options. The ultimate decision as to the form of the permanent government is the population's choice. This is a process that could take years or generations.

In every society, leaders evolve. That should be encouraged. Those individuals and groups that show an aptitude for government should be brought into the government as early as possible. There is one caveat. They must be trained, and they must demonstrate a belief that the interest of the general society comes before their interest. This is the idealistic philosophy that must be present. Unfortunately, it is common knowledge that some of the leaders of some of the Western democracies do not always subscribe to that philosophy within their own state.

Starting on an elementary scale, the local people that have been brought into the government can be trained for minor roles in the local, regional and national government. As progress is made, they can be guided into positions of increased responsibility and thereby gradually replacing UGSP/UN administrators.

During this entire process of transition, the UGSP/UN guided government shall keep an increasingly literate population informed of the progress. The UGSP/UN shall be training the native administrators and educating the populace toward the day when they are capable of choosing the type government that the society believes best suits their needs.

Before we leave this section there should be a discussion of the issue of a society that is more suited to a monarchy or a religious government. That grates on Western thinking even though much of Europe's rise to prominence was with monarchs and/or heavily influenced by religion.

It has been stated that a careful study must be made of the state's political history and its political aptitude. If prior to the global-security-threatening problem the state had a history of a basically satisfied society governed by a monarch, it is possible that the monarchy should be restored. It is possible that there are members of the ruling family, that have the society's interest foremost, who could be returned to power. That government should, however, be encouraged to become a constitutional monarchy. The same can be said for a state which was governed by a religion. The problem here, of course, is convincing the religious leaders that they must be tolerant of other religions within the society. We must remember that many societies know no other form of government. If a given society has the necessary access to education and freedom of expression, it is possible that over time, like most Western states, that society will re-invent itself into a democracy. However, that is their choice, not the choice of the UGSP.

EIGHT: THE UNITED GLOBAL SECURITY PARTNERSHIP SHALL INSURE THAT ECONOMIC AND SOCIAL DEVELOPMENT SHALL CONTINUE DURING OCCUPATION. THIS SHALL BE CONSISTANT WITH LOCAL VALUES AND GOALS. WHERE POSSIBLE, THE NATIONAL DEVELOPMENT GOALS WILL BE FUNDED FROM LOCAL INDUSTRIAL AND NATURAL RESOURCES.

To move the occupied state on the path to economic and social development there will be two goals: 1) Guide the government along a progression for the return to self-rule. 2) The occupied state will be returned to the world community of healthy and productive states.

Afghanistan is an excellent example of the problems of abandoning a state after the initial problem is solved, thus leaving an ill-equipped country to fend for itself. The United States and the West supplied the Afghan freedom fighters against the Soviet Union. Those freedom fighters were composed of tribes that normally warred against each other. As soon as the Soviet Union withdrew and Western interest waned, those tribes began quarreling again. This made for a fertile ground for the incursion of an opportunistic group. That group was the Taliban. The Taliban is a group consisting primarily of Pashtun tribal members or those supported by the Pashtun. They came in from Pakistan. While their rule was oppressive, they offered stability to a war weary people. The Taliban gave support to and harbored the al Qaeda international terrorist organization.

After 9-11 the United States led a campaign to remove the Taliban from Afghan rule. After that effort was successfully completed the United States shifted its focus to Iraq, whereupon al Qaeda and the Taliban were able to regroup. The problem of Afghanistan became far greater than it had been. In short, had the West not all but abandoned Afghanistan, the face of international terrorism in the first decades of the twenty-first century might have been much different.

The Taliban spent a lot of propaganda effort in "educating" the population as to the evils of all who opposed them. Much of that propaganda damage, as well as their terrorist campaign, has "spilled over" to other states, other terrorist groups, religious groups and societies.

It is reasonable that when the UGSP gains control there will be a preconceived mistrust or even hatred for the occupying UGSP and its administrating force. That mistrust or hatred will be both within the occupied state and within the other groups that have been influenced who reside outside that state. The attention of the entire world will be focused on the occupation. It is therefore extremely important that the rebuilding be accomplished compassionately and with an obvious absence of any self-serving or selfish motive. It must be clearly demonstrated from the outset of the occupation that the problem group or government's propaganda was a lie.

Just as this work has attempted to make clear that no one state can afford to be the "world's policeman", neither can the UGSP effectively fulfill all the mandates of this work. It must have help and cooperation from other agencies. For example, under a UN umbrella, the World Health Organization, the World Bank and probably the ICC will be key participants in the reconstruction. The special skills of other organizations should be employed as needed. For purposes of this discussion this work will use the UN as the lead agency.

Even before the UGSP has occupied and secured the problem state, the UGSP should organize the reconstruction team. By so doing, the UN and the initial occupying government will be able to be in business almost immediately upon occupation. The first social priorities are the immediate needs for feeding, housing, healthcare and clothing. Apart from the obvious humanitarian considerations, meeting those immediate needs will help with stabilization, trust and cooperation. These measures are not the long term solutions to these needs. It will require careful study and planning to effect the long term solutions. Rather, these measures are about relieving the immediate suffering.

The UGSP/UN should utilize experts in all the disciplines which affect the occupied state as members of the reconstruction team. That is, individuals and organizations who are experts in the history and religion(s) of the occupied state, the governmental structure that the population understands, the scope and levels of education of the population. Team members must include experts in the fields of medicine, education, urban and rural planning and housing. Team members must also include experts on the economic situation and the economic possibilities of the occupied state. They must have a clear knowledge of the natural, agricultural, industrial and technological resources and capabilities of the state. There will need to be members who can assess the monetary requirements during reconstruction and whether those requirements must be met through "foreign aid", long term loans, domestic production or a combination of some or all.

It will be important to include individuals or groups from within the population to assist and render advice. Try as they might, a native of cities such as Chicago or London or Berlin cannot possibly understand all of the subtleties of societies in states such as Nigeria or Bora Bora for example. It is important that, where possible, policies are put in place that are non-offensive. To offend even the subtleties can damage the quest for trust and cooperation. This list is not meant to be complete. Each situation will be different and require different or more or less team members. However, the point is made.

From this group and with local input, the reconstruction plan shall be made. Each of the team members shall clearly understand their mission and goals. The UN shall then appoint a commission to oversee and coordinate those missions. The UGSP, while still maintaining ultimate control, should no longer be needed on a day to day managerial level. That lack of direct need for the UGSP could extend to, if appropriate, the occupying military security force. If possible, it would be desirable to have the occupying military force consist of personnel of similar ethnic, social and/or religious background.

Great emphasis must be placed upon education with the goal of a maximum percentage of the population achieving literacy. No society in the world has a one hundred percent literacy rate. However, it is no secret that the more widespread and higher the level of education, the less vulnerable a population is to outside negative influence. With widespread literacy a society has a better ability to make thoughtful decisions.

At the elementary level, besides teaching the basics of education, the ability to think independently and creatively should be encouraged and re-enforced. By so doing, the desire for higher education will be more prevalent. That will be the nation's source of future leaders in business, government and social organizations. All people are not college material, but all people should have the opportunity to gain the skills they require in order to be productive. Trade schools and apprentice programs should be established. They should be geared to local economic and resource conditions. For example, little would be accomplished by educating mining engineers in a state with few mineral resources and an economy naturally based upon fishing.

While the state's education system is being developed and thereafter, students that demonstrate great aptitude in a field should be provided generous scholarships to study abroad at the appropriate institute. Those scholarships should carry the caveat that upon completion of the study, the students will return to their native state and practice that discipline for a specified period of time. That service can be satisfied either within the government structure or in a private enterprise or practice. Several things will be accomplished by this policy:

1. Those individuals will contribute to the health and growth of their state.
2. They will have had the chance to witness first-hand the benefits of other developed states and return home with ideas.
3. By providing these educational and professional opportunities, the benevolence of the UGSP and the UN will have again been demonstrated.

It is important that as the education level improves, those "native" people appropriately educated must be integrated into the system. They must be able to be employed in those fields with the long term goal of individual self-sufficiency. Besides building self-sufficiency and pride, self-respect will be fostered and the increased employment will help rebuild the state's economic base.

The UGSP and the UN should be developing and training a national military, local and national police and a judiciary. The military should be in the form of a militia to maintain internal security and to insure the safety of the population. It must not be a trained, aggressive force to be utilized beyond the borders. The goal here is to gradually replace UGSP, or other foreign military forces placed in the state by the UGPS, with a local militia that the population can trust. The same is true of training local police to handle the day to day criminal activities that occur in any society. That native police force must be trained with long term principles of fair treatment to instill trust by the citizenry. It may be possible to immediately seat local, native magistrates. If that is possible, so much the better. However, the UGSP/UN must promote the education of capable people in the law so that, at the earliest possible time, the state is handling its own legal affairs.

A careful analysis of the state's agricultural and industrial capabilities and its natural resources must be made. A plan must be designed for the intelligent utilization and development of those resources. If those resources are in capable, private, non-exploitive hands, they should remain so. "Non-exploitive hands" means the fair treatment and compensation of labor and the marketplace.

The occupation of Afghanistan offers an interesting example. The United States put in place an "Alternative Development and Livelihoods Program". That program was designed to provide for "immediate needs" and "cash-for-work" sponsoring labor intensive work projects to rehabilitate agricultural infrastructure such as drainage and irrigation canals. The program also provided for agricultural development initiatives, credit and financial services. However, those programs needed to be tightly controlled. For example, from 2002 through 2008, 'cash-for-work' paid out $37 million dollars to farmers who might otherwise have engaged in opium poppies."[1] Creating a state of security, which would encourage foreign investment could change that dynamic, create jobs, and provide revenue for the government.

Afghanistan has incredible economic potential. The U. S. Geological Survey, building and expanding on the old Soviet explorations, estimated the mineral wealth of Afghanistan at probably over one trillion dollars. The Afghan Minister of Mines, Wahidullah Shahnani, put the number closer to three trillion dollars.[2]

It is estimated that there is over two billion metric tons of iron, the largest deposits in the world, over 62 percent of the world total. They have large deposits of copper, cobalt, lithium, topaz, emeralds, rubies and lapis lazuli. There may well be 1.8 billion barrels of crude oil and ample natural gas deposits. To date, only 30 percent of the country has been explored. Afghanistan is strategically located for a potential oil and gas transit pipeline"[3]

If the United States can create a secure environment in Afghanistan it may be possible to attract more investment. There will be more than enough money for infrastructure building, education, job creation, health care, and last but not least, taking care of the government. The Afghan government has contracted with a few companies for the exploration and development of natural resources in Bamyam Province."(4) Not all states that need to be occupied have the natural resources potential that are present in Afghanistan. Nonetheless, the point is made.

Careful consideration must also be given to the intelligent planning for the long term utilization of the resource with environmental considerations factored into the mix. If the private ownership of those resources cannot, or is not willing to meet the basic criteria, they should be compensated and the resource nationalized until the state has developed people who are capable of sound management. At that time the resource should be returned to private enterprise. There are any number of generally accepted ways of accomplishing the return to private ownership. Some of those methods include public stock corporations, privately held corporations and low interest loans. In any event, the nationalization of enterprises and the transfer to private ownership must be very public and transparent with competitive proposals submitted by qualified independent individuals or groups.

It is recognized that the determination of what resources are important enough to be of concern to the UN and UGSP is a complicated matter. Again, each situation will be different and it would be presumptuous to attempt to set out definite guidelines in this work. Hopefully, common sense, a sense of fairness and practical thinking will prevail at the time. For example, if labor is being treated as slave labor with clear violations of worldwide, commonly accepted child labor considerations, that enterprise needs supervision. If the labor problem consist of a dispute over day-care, that is a problem that can probably be left to the parties and the national (or local) judicial system which the UGSP/UN should be developing.

If the state has large reserves of iron ore with significant national economic and environmental impacts, the UGSP and the UN should be concerned. A local fishing cooperative should probably be left alone unless it is over-fishing the supply. If an enterprise is belching massive amounts of hydrocarbons into the air or massive amounts of toxic materials into the water system, it should be of concern. On the other hand, minor environmental problems can be solved by those affected or the judiciary.

When and where possible, the direct cost of the removal of the global threatening situation, the occupation and administration of the problem state should be financed from local resources. Here again, a great deal of care must be taken. One must remember that, in most cases, the surviving population is as much the victim as the world order, if not more so. Only the direct cost of the operation may be considered. While it may be complicated and difficult to identify all the direct costs, the basic ones can be identified. Costs such as fuel and ammunition can be ascertained. The cost of housing, feeding and clothing within the state of both the administrators and the population can also be determined. Buying the states of the UGSP a fleet of new warplanes or ships, aside from those that may have been lost in the battle for control, is not a legitimate direct cost.

It was stated earlier in this section that experts in the monetary needs of the occupation and reconstruction are required. Those experts must be able to determine and develop a plan for the monetary contribution by the state toward the direct costs of control, occupation and reconstruction. That plan must not be punitive to the emerging state's economic recovery. It must first make certain that economic resources are providing for the population and fueling the growth necessary for the goal of self-rule and self-sufficiency. After those considerations have been met, and only after those considerations been met, should reimbursements be made to the UGSP and the UN.

CHAPTER EIGHT

THE POLITICAL CONSEQUENCES: "WINNING THE HEARTS AND MINDS"

While winning the "hearts and minds" of the population is certainly vitally important, the first priority is removing the actual or potential threat to world security. If that can be done with local resources, under UGSP supervision, the political damage could be minimized. In the case of the presence of terrorist groups in an otherwise co-operative state, if deemed prudent by the UGSP, the existing government could be protected from instability until calm and order are restored.

The problem with the Iraq/Kuwait "Desert Storm" operation was that it was a United States led coalition rather than a permanent coalition of a select group of committed states. The United States employed excellent diplomatic finesse. Even so, the United States had great difficulty putting together and holding together a coalition of states against Iraq. Many of those states were not natural United States allies. In fact, several of them could be characterized as United States adversaries. However, in joining the coalition, those states saw their immediate national interest as being more important than their long term problems with the United States.

Many pundits criticized the United States for not taking the "Desert Storm" fight to the end and removing the Iraqi regime headed by Saddam Hussein. The political climate in the Middle East in 1991 would have made such an action dangerous. Many of the states in the Middle East would have viewed that action as excessive and as the attempted "conquest" of a fellow Arab state or a fight against Islam. That continued action could have laid the seeds of hatred for the United States for years or generations to come. It could also have laid the seeds for continued violence and conflict in the area for generations to come. Those two problems were yet to come in the aftermath of the 2003 re-invasion of Iraq.

Again, the primary problem is that the coalition was not permanent and the United States cannot continue to be the "policeman" of the world essentially alone. While it is not the purview of this study, the turmoil which followed the ultimate removal of Hussein demonstrates the need for extensive research and planning for the aftermath of an action.

It has been stated that the seeds of future conflict are sown by the way one executes the current action. The massive high tech targeting of only legitimate military targets should minimize civilian casualties and make it safer for occupying UGSP forces.

If a general population within a state feels they have been grossly violated one has enormous long term problems. This is also true if the populations of other surrounding states share the same philosophy as the belligerents, and they also believe they have been grossly violated. In both cases there are enormous long term problems. We have witnessed the validity of the consequences of poor planning or overreach in the aftermath of the 2003 invasion of Iraq.

Careful consideration must be given by the UGSP as to the long term political consequences of its planned action on the general population, surrounding states and groups. That consideration must be made within the UGSP's secret planning before the course of action is announced. This means that great consideration must be given to the minimizing of civilian casualties. Plans must be made to render assistance to the population, if possible, during the action. In short, great emphasis must be placed on compassion both during and after the action. Consideration must be given and a well thought-out plan must be formed as to the long term social, economic and political consequences for the non-combatants. If the population is left to suffer or their well-being left to chance, the long term problems could become unmanageable.

People and societies have long memories when it comes to such things, and they can nurture grudges for years or, in some cases, for centuries. Some of the possibly irreparable animosities in the Balkans in today's twenty-first century go back to ethnic massacres that took place in the thirteenth and fourteenth centuries. A society that feels it has been grossly violated becomes fertile ground for a subsequent "rogue" individual or rogue group.

It is appropriate to discuss successes and failures in the fight to win the "hearts and minds" of a population by the state or coalition of states that defeated that population's ruling regime.

While one could not characterize "Desert Storm" as a major success in the winning of "hearts and minds", at least very little damage was done. There were limited civilian casualties because of the planning and execution. Therefore, there has been very little criticism of the action. The action was limited to its stated goal: the removal of Iraq from Kuwait. No one could fault the coalition for overstepping its power and becoming the aggressor.

Parts of the coalition (the United States and Great Britain) continued through limited air power in the northern and southern parts of Iraq to enforce "no fly" zones. This was to attempt to protect elements within the Iraqi population, such as the Northern Kurds, from the oppression of the Iraqi regime. That enforcement of the no fly zones was also designed to limit the Iraqi ability to mount an ambitious adventure. There was some criticism of the United States/British enforcement, but that was tempered by some level of comfort in neighboring states and the well documented previous aggression by the Iraqi regime against their own people. However, it should be emphasized that by enforcing the "no fly" zones, the United States and Great Britain committed themselves to a costly, open ended operation with no end in sight.

Early in this work there was a discussion of the treatment of Germany after its defeat in World War One as an example of an earlier failure. The Allies were so focused upon revenge that the terms of surrender at Versailles and the demands for reparations were so oppressive that the Allies believed that Germany's weakness was assured. The seeds of discontent were successfully sown. It is no wonder, in hindsight, that the Nazis were so successful in stirring the German people and organizing them into a very efficient, aggressive military power.

Every lie must have a germ of truth to be credible. In Germany's case, the germ of truth was the Allied treatment of defeated World War One Germany. Given Germany's sorry state, the need of the German people for order and their work ethic guaranteed the emergence of a new and powerful German state.

The Nazi lie about the Jewish "threat" had very little credibility, unless one considers as a threat some Jews being successful members of the professional and merchant class. However, given the dire condition of the German people, the campaigns of the Nazis and the creation by the Nazis of a "scapegoat", made the Jews an easy target. The people needed someone to hate to get "fired up".

Contrast the treatment of Germany at the end of World War One with its treatment by the Allies at the end of World War Two. Germany was included fully in the rebuilding of Europe. The economic and humanitarian aid given by the Allies (primarily the United States) created a German state that is a civilized and willing ally of the powers that defeated it in World War Two. This is an example of an unqualified success.

Another failure was the division of land demanded by the Soviet Union and the states that therefore fell under Soviet domination at the end of World War Two. Over the years those states were unable to mount successful rebellions even though there was continuous resistance. The Soviet Union was only able to retain control through its military and police-state oppression which was ultimately a crippling expense. The Soviet oppressive tactics and policies not only did not win the hearts and minds but insured a sometimes not so quiet resentment. The astonishingly rapid collapse of the Soviet Union and its loss of grip on the "satellite" states could, in part, be attributed to this treatment and the subsequent resentment.

The creation of the modern state of Israel was a messy affair. It was to be divided into two states, the modern state of Israel and a Palestinian homeland with defined borders. The UN endorsed that division. The Palestinians rejected it. The history is far more complicated. However, one thing should be painfully clear. It was a major failure in the securing of the hearts and minds of all parties concerned. The Western powers did not sufficiently weigh the long term consequences of creating this division of land.

Palestine was a British mandate until May, 1948. The Balfour Declaration of 1917 favored a separate homeland for Jews and Palestinians. President Roosevelt assured the Arabs of no U. S. intervention without consulting both Arabs and Jews. Yet President Truman endorsed the creation of Israel which the British opposed. The first Israeli/Arab war broke out immediately after the announcement of the State of Israel on May 14, 1948.(1)

That is not to mean in any way that the modern state of Israel should not have been created. Rather, it means that greater study of the long term impact on the region and the well-being of all should have held a much higher degree of importance. The fact that the Arab states and societies in the Middle East vowed, from the outset, to "drive the Jews (Zionist) into the sea", should have sent the planners and diplomats "back to the drawing board". The deep resentments stemming from that action have caused, to date, nearly three quarters of a century of conflict, violence and hatred. It is very likely that even with a resolution of the Israeli/Palestinian issue and the creation thereby of a Palestinian state or homeland, at the very least the underlying conflicts, violence and hatreds may never end. Certainly it will take a long time for any kind of trust to develop.

The consequences of not understanding the resentments of the people in the region has caused widespread violence beyond the immediate borders.

It has created vast ideological rifts nearly worldwide, and has the potential to escalate into world conflict. This is not to say that the Israeli/Palestinian conflict is solely responsible for the conflicts between the West and some of the Arab world. For a variety of reasons those problems would still occur. However, it certainly plays a part and is a ready excuse (every lie must have a germ of truth to be believable) for people of dubious ambition. Over the years the West has exacerbated the situation by not ascertaining (or ignoring), yet again, the long term consequences of their actions on the regional societies.

It has been discussed above that each situation would be different. There will be different politics, different problem groups, different geography, rural versus urban, etc. After the September, 2001 World Trade Center attack the United States put together yet another temporary coalition to rid Afghanistan of its Taliban government which had supported the al-Qaeda terrorist network. That network is believed to be responsible for the September, 2001, terrorist attack upon the United States. After the removal of the Taliban government, the United States shifted its attention to Iraq. That gave the Taliban and al Qaeda an opportunity to regroup, strengthen and foment resentment and even hatred for the West with much of the population.

Afghanistan is in the same part of the world as Iraq, yet the problems and their solutions were vastly different in both situations. In the case of Iraq, there was an easily located regime. The Iraqi regime of Saddam Hussein was well located and identified both politically and geographically. With the Taliban and al-Qaeda terrorist networks, their location and structure in Afghanistan, and the world, was and is shadowy and allusive.

In the "Desert Storm" operation against Iraq, while much of the precise surgical elimination of many of the military targets was in urbanized areas, much of the actions took place in essentially a desert environment. In Afghanistan, many of the targets are in urbanized areas with high civilian populations as well as mountainous terrain and safe havens across the border in Pakistan. Therefore, unlike Iraq, the situation in Afghanistan from a military standpoint became impossible. The enemy, while poorly equipped by Western standards, is determined, dedicated and seasoned. The Taliban and al Qaeda fostered a hatred for the West, America in particular, with much of the population of Afghanistan.

The massive, precise, overwhelming use of high tech weaponry has not broken the will of the Taliban and al-Qaeda. It did break the will of the Iraqi army. However, at this writing, Iraq is still a hotbed of internal strife and terrorism. Moreover, in both Iraq and Afghanistan, the struggles will not come to a successful conclusion without the co-operation of the people. That can only be achieved by security, social services and government reforms. It is interesting to note that the United States did have a measure of favor during the long drawn out conflict wherein Afghan warlords, with the help from Pakistan's Inter-Service Intelligence (ISI) and the U. S CIA, drove the Soviet Union out in defeat over a ten year period.

The point of this last discussion is to further point out that each situation is different and requires learned planning on the part of the UGSP. The United States-led coalition going against the Taliban and al-Qaeda has tried to utilize some of the same tactics as were used in Iraq. Surgical bombing has led to some good successes. Unfortunately, the planners did not understand the strong tribal allegiances or the role Afghan heroin plays in funding al Qaeda and the Taliban terrorism. Additionally, in the West and in the United States, the United States led coalition has not made a strong enough case in the court of public opinion for the fact that this will not be as easy as Iraq was in Desert Storm. As a result, the world expected a quick resolution in Afghanistan and some of the Arab states and members of the coalition demanded a quick cessation of the military action.

Because of the nature of the enemy, its shadowy existence and the terrain, in order to minimize civilian and coalition casualties, this battle will be a lengthy one. The coalition must step up its information campaign to educate the region and the world as to the complexity of the problem. Additionally, they must continue their effort to counter the Taliban and al

Qaeda. Afghanistan is a good example of the need to recognize the desperate state of the civilian population. That recognition is being addressed by the coalition. There is a real chance to win the hearts and minds through the deliverance of continued aid to the population. It would also be a great help if the government of Afghanistan would live up to its promises as to the deliverance of security and social services. The coalition must also force the government to eliminate corruption.

The conflict in Iraq and the quagmire in Afghanistan have caused public opinion to favor planned withdrawals of forces. Whether or not those withdrawals are prudent remains to be seen. In Iraq, the vacuum that troop withdrawal and governmental corruption created the emergence of the Islamic State in Iraq and Syria (ISIS) which now in 2015 is a major problem.

In Afghanistan the planned withdrawal of troops may create a renewed opportunity for al Qaeda and the Taliban to reverse the gains of the American led coalition. Both situations in Iraq and Afghanistan emphasize the need for considering the long-term consequences of any enforcement action.

As the local population and the world see the high degree of humanitarian aid sponsored by the UGSP and the UN, with a concurrent diminishing of control of the government by the UGSP, the UGSP's credibility should increase. The world will understand that the stated mission of the UGSP is purely world peace and security. The world will understand that the UGSP is not another militarily powerful consortium of ambitious states.

From the outset of this work it has been stated that the basic idea of a world police force is offensive to the thinking of most people and to most states. However, if the issue of state sovereignty can be resolved and if the world sees a UGSP strictly adhering to its stated enforcement plan to protect world security and to bring the problem state to a productive member of the world community, with no other agenda, world acceptance and approval just might be achieved.

CHAPTER NINE

SHARED RESPONSIBILITY

In order to achieve initial tolerance and long term acceptance by the world community of states, the UGSP must incorporate the UN, the ICJ, and the ICC in the overall concept.

The UN would be the co-administrators of occupied problem states and the provider of all the necessary humanitarian aid. The ICJ would continue to attempt to solve disputes between states. The ICC would be the dispenser of justice to the responsible parties threating world security. While each of these entities has been discussed earlier, let us now review the responsibilities of each of these four organizations.

The role of the United Global Security Partnership

As to the primary role of the UGSP, one is referred back to the eight principles outlined in Chapter Seven.

In the event, and the events will occur, where a member state of the UGSP has economic or political interest in the state(s) which is the subject of possible UGSP interdiction, that member state shall put aside its interest or recuse itself from that particular action. It is hopeful that the member state will realize that its long term interest may be better served by doing so.

An excellent example of the above protocol is the case of Iraq's economic relationship with the Russian Federation in the last decade of the twentieth century and the first decade of the twenty-first century. In this time period, Iraq owed a major financial debt to Russia, and Russia needed Iraqi oil. However, Iraq posed a major threat to world security. Iraq was in a position to export significant terrorist problems to states which border the Russian Federation and to the Russian Federation itself. Chechnya comes immediately to mind. Being a part of the UGSP or cooperating with a UGSP solution to the Iraqi problem would not have prevented the Russian Federation from engaging in a renewed economic relationship with Iraq after a settlement of the Iraqi problem. Additionally, a terrorist threat would have been removed from the Russian Federation borders.

The UGSP must be "blind" as to the form of government, social institutions and religions of all states. Even if those institutions are repugnant to most societies the UGSP will not interfere with the strictly internal affairs of any state. Nor will the UGSP use those institutions which are repugnant as an excuse to manufacture a world crisis. Before any action is contemplated, clear evidence of a potential international crisis must be present. The sovereignty of all states shall be respected until they threaten the sovereignty of other states.

To whatever degree possible, the member states of the UGSP shall represent the greatest diversity of geography, religions and political points of view. This will go a long way toward achieving world acceptance and help insure the fairness of UGSP actions. That diversity must be tempered with the recognition by the member states that they will not let their religious views hamper enforcement within a problem state which shares the same religious position.

One of the great benefits of the diversity of the member states is that there are several capable states in the world at the beginning of the twenty-first century that have been either enemies or have held strong suspicions of one another. The rivalry between the United States, the old USSR (with residual suspicions by the Russian Federation) and China are good examples. All of these states recognize the advantages of security and economic development. If they were now in a global security partnership, providing joint planning and security in a spirit of cooperation, those suspicions and animosities might be resolved or at the very least be manageable.

The independence of the UGSP is essential or the concept is for naught. If the UGSP had to seek the permission of other organizations before initiating an enforcement, it is quite likely that the UGSP would be ineffectual. This does not mean, however, that the UGSP will act capriciously. It will conduct a thorough investigation. It will notify the target state or group and the world at large of its investigation. It will seek, but not be bound by, expert testimony and advice from other appropriate individuals, groups, states and organizations.

The UPGS will occupy a problem state only so long as it takes to bring about a lasting security. At the point in time when the problem state can return to the productive community of states, the UGSP shall leave and that state shall have total sovereignty.

The role of the United Nations

With the UGSP in place, the UN could provide the UGSP with support during the occupation of a problem state in the form of a "peacekeeping" role. However, because the UN has proved to be less than effective in the role of "preventing breaches to world security" the UN should relinquish that primary role to the UGSP.

The UN should retain the Security Council. The Security Council of the UN could be of great assistance to the UGSP. It could help identify problem situations. It could help with advice to the UGSP. Conceivably, member states of the Security Council could persuade problem states over which they have influence, to correct the problem and thus avoid UGSP intervention. These actions by the Security Council could also lend credibility to the UGSP.

As the UGSP is formulating the plan of action to solve a world security threatening problem, it should involve the UN. The UN should be the lead agency for the administration of the humanitarian needs and the reconstruction of the problem state. These are the functions for which the UN is best suited. These are the functions which will prevent the abandonment of the problem state after the conflict has been resolved. These, too, are the functions which will demonstrate to the world that peace and reconstruction are the only objectives. These are the functions that will help win the hearts and minds of the population, thus reversing, albeit possibly very slowly, a vicious and dangerous mindset.

As a result of the partnership with the UN, the involvement of the UGSP in the affairs of the occupied state can be minimized. This will help give the states of the world a sense of confidence that the motives of the UGSP are purely world security and not an attempt to dominate. As long as the preplanned goals are on track, the UGSP can limit its involvement to overseeing security. This will allow the UN to do its job unhampered. This partnership with the UN in the administration of the problem state will also help minimize the drain on UGSP member state's resources.

The role of the International Court of Justice (the World Court)

The World Court is also more officially known as the International Court of Justice (ICJ). It is a part of the UN.

A few facts concerning the International Court of Justice (ICJ) are in order before the discussion of the role of the ICJ is presented. It was formed in 1946 and it replaced the Permanent Court of International Justice. Its principal role was, and should remain, the attempt to settle or mediate disputes between states. These disputes are more "civil" in nature. For example, they may involve alleged treaty violations. The fifteen judges are elected by the UN General Assembly and the Security Council. They serve nine-year terms. The ICJ is headquartered in The Hague.

Over the years the ICJ has not been as effective as one would hope. There are two primary problems for the ICJ. First, states must voluntarily agree to be subject to the ICJ's jurisdiction and abide by its rulings. If one of the parties does not abide by the ruling, the only recourse for the other party is an appeal to the UN Security Council. The record is not very clear as to Security Council action. Second, the ICJ has no effective enforcement vehicle.

If states could agree to be bound by the rulings of the ICJ some disputes between states could be settled before violence ensues. The dispute between Great Britain and Argentina over the Falkland Islands comes quickly to mind. In fact, states of the world should be encouraged to bring their cases before the ICJ. Disputes such as trade disagreements could be decided by the ICJ and the honoring of its decision left to the states involved. However, if one state defaults on an agreed upon settlement, the UGSP could intervene if it deems intervention is warranted. This author has no illusions as to the difficulty that agreement between states presents.

The role of the International Criminal Court (ICC)

The Rome Statute of the International Criminal Court established the ICC in 1998.

The ICC should be completely independent of the UGSP. While co-operating with the UN, the ICC should be separate from the UN. The ICC should be the organization that administers justice to the perpetrators of the global threatening problem. In order to make justice even handed in the eyes of the world, the justices, for which eighteen are elected, must not come from any of the member states of the UGSP. The Charter of the ICC is structurally sound. It provides for the impartiality of the justices and an equitable geographic origin of the justices.

As the ICJ should be able to mediate disputes between states which are "civil" in nature, the ICC has jurisdiction over disputes that are the result of armed conflict or could result in armed conflict. The ICC has jurisdiction over *individuals* who threaten world security or commit crimes against humanity. That jurisdiction should be expanded to include *states* that commit crimes against humanity. Disputes that could very likely result in armed conflict could have the decision of the ICC enforced by the UGSP. Unlike most courts in most states who can call on law enforcement, neither the ICJ nor the ICC have an effective enforcement arm. Granted, if the state from which an accused criminal suspect agrees, and only if that state agrees to ICC jurisdiction, the ICC has the power of arrest and imprisonment. As difficult as it would be to establish, all states should be obligated to adhere to ICC jurisdiction. With the UGSP in place, the ICC would have a vastly expanded enforcement capability. As with any world security-threatening situation, the UGSP would employ its usual investigative process before enforcing a ruling of the ICC.

In order to have the widest range of input in the decision making process the justices of the ICC have a "Prosecutor" who has the power to gather evidence. The Prosecutor is able to impanel a group of experts knowledgeable about the dispute or the trial of individuals before the Court.

It has earlier been stated that the ICC proceedings in the cases of perpetrators and accomplices in the conflict or terrorist acts should be conducted with a limited amount of press coverage. This is not to imply that the trials should be secret with no public accountability. Rather, it is to prevent the opportunity for "grandstanding", the giving of a public forum to the accused individuals. The war crimes trial of Slobodan Milosevic, the president of Serbia from 1989 through 1997, exemplifies the need for the limits on press coverage. Public martyrdom for the individuals involved would be far less than desirable.

In the field, the UGSP may be able to determine those individuals who were nothing more than "foot soldiers". Those individuals will be disarmed and sent home. Their identities shall be noted and their treatment will be different if they appear again. Those whom the UGSP determines present a threat or are perpetrators and accomplices shall be held in custody and their cases shall be determined by the ICC. As previously stated, a death sentence in some cases will be warranted. It is a legitimate sentence that should be invoked in some cases without hesitation. It should be widely known throughout the world that if one does the crime, death could very likely be the punishment. It has often been stated that the death penalty is not a deterrent. It is this author's opinion that if the death penalty is not a deterrent, it is because that form of justice is so slow in coming. It is so unevenly administered, that many criminals do not believe they will suffer the fate. If, however, the ICC, and local courts for that matter, set out the criteria for the imposition of the death penalty and they adhere to it in a timely manner, the likelihood of the death penalty will be a lesson and a deterrent.

In some cases, even the most evil of rogues would be better left alive. This is particularly true if they could provide valuable ongoing information regarding terrorist cells, their location, the individuals involved, their financing, their mission and activities. In these cases, if the death penalty is warranted, the ICC could suspend the sentence, well documenting their reasoning, in order to secure the cooperation of the condemned. That cooperation could result in a commutation to life imprisonment.

Where the ICC has sentenced certain individuals to prison terms, under the UGSP those prison terms shall be served in cooperating states *other* than the states that are member states of the UGSP. This third party incarceration shall further reassure the world of the lack of desire on the part of the UGSP to dominate. Upon release, second offenses shall be dealt with severely. Unfortunately, as with common criminals, incarceration can be a badge of glory and esteem for some political rebels. That cannot be allowed to happen. They must know that, as a condition of release or probation, they will never again engage in the activity that caused their imprisonment. They must be assured and convinced of the severity of the punishment for a repeat offense.

Restating, by the inclusion of the UN, the ICJ and the ICC in the UGSP agenda, the states of the world will feel they have some voice in the concept of the enforcement of world peace. That might initially cause them to tolerate the structure. The long term acceptance will result from the coordinated, carefully planned action of the UGSP, the UN, the ICJ and the ICC and the fair treatment of the offending parties.

It is interesting that the world already has the basic building blocks for this thesis. There is a UN, albeit flawed. There is an ICJ and there is an ICC. However, as has been noted, the existing courts have little or no enforcement capability. There are security organizations such as NATO and SEATO which, unfortunately, are reactive rather than proactive and are geographically oriented. There are coalitions formed from time to time to resolve world security threats. It would not take much other than the will of states and intelligent planning to take the next steps to initiate this thesis for the permanent creation of the UGSP along with the redirection of the mission of the UN, the ICJ and the ICC.

CHAPTER TEN

FUNDING THE UNITED GLOBAL SECURITY PARTNERSHIP

Nearly all states in the world have a military, either great or small and, therefore, military expense. For too many states that military budget takes a disproportionate percentage of their Gross National Product (GNP). This is true of the world's great powers as well as the weaker states. The old Soviet Union is a good example. While there were other major, basic flaws in the Soviet economic system, the inordinately high level of military "defense" spending robbed the state of much needed economic resources. That contributed to the collapse of the Soviet Union. It has been said that the United States forced the Soviets into an ever-increasing, unsustainable arms spending race. That may or may not be true. What is a fact, however, is that the Soviet Union could not afford their military.

The United States is a very productive state with an enormous amount of economic power. It is a state that, in the beginning of the twenty-first century, is able to sustain its military. In fact, in times of crises the United States can call on vast economic reserves. The United States is confident of its ability, its power and its proven capability to exercise that power in a time of crisis. The United States may be too confident. There is some sobering precedence.

It has been stated repeatedly in this work that no state can afford an ever-expanding empire. It has been the historic norm for the great powers to expand their influence and control to the point at which they can no longer sustain the economic burden.(1) That has led to either their collapse or the reduction of their power to that of the second or third tier of states. In the last decade of the twentieth century and at the opening of the twenty-first century it appears that possibly the United States may not be able to sustain its high level of commitments. The United States does not appear to be heeding this lesson of history. While the United States has partners in conflicts, occasionally different partners in different conflicts, the Unites States carries a disproportionate share of the load. The United States appears to do so willingly. Just as with the other prior "super power" states of the world, the United States will find itself spending more on defense to be the "world policeman" than it can afford.

States support a military for two reasons: 1) if they are so inclined, states will support a military for aggressive purposes and; 2) states will support a military for the defense against threats either real or feared, justified or unjustified.

A primary goal of an effective UGSP would be that aggressive states would not be able to spend the money for a large military force because they would have already been admonished and warned by the UGSP. Recognition of that goal could meet with some resistance. If states have been checked in their aggressive ambitions their neighbors will have a lesser need to fund a large defensive force. These states will be able to channel financial assets into other more productive projects.

The states who are willing and capable member states of the UGSP may find that for UGSP missions, their combined and centrally controlled military power is more effective and smaller in quantity than the total of their current individual armed forces. It may be possible for the individual member states of the UGSP to fund the organization with a smaller contribution than each of them currently spends on their individual militaries. Simply put, each member state maintains its own military. That military is available to the UGSP. Because of the combined alliance of the UGSP member states, each member state may be able to field a smaller, less expensive military. Additionally, as the UGSP proves effective through decisive actions, international threats should decrease, further reducing each state's need for large militaries

It should be noted that states have been reluctant to place their military under "foreign" leadership in a time of crisis. In fact, currently the United States has a policy of not placing its military under foreign command. In most of the world conflicts in modern times in which "foreign" leadership has been employed it has met with varying degrees of success. More to the point, through extensive training and joint exercises of the combined UGSP forces, greater confidence in the military leadership abilities of each of the member states can be achieved.

It is unrealistic to believe that the states of the world who are not member states of UGSP could be "taxed" to support the UGSP. Besides sovereignty issues, they just will not do it. There is, therefore, no point in entertaining the prospect. There are, however, other possibilities for funding the UGSP besides the member states funding the UGSP on their own.

If the UGSP is effective in controlling world conflicts the UN would be relieved of much of its "peacekeeping" responsibilities. It has been recommended in this work that the UN contribute to the ongoing peacekeeping of occupied states. The UGSP's initial resolution of the threat would relieve the UN of the expense of funding an armed force to quell the conflict. Some of that savings could be contributed to the cost of the UGSP's operation. Those UN contributions must come with no "strings". That is, the UN cannot condition the funding on actions, or inactions, of the UGSP which are desired by the UN. That caveat obviously holds true for any funding source. The UGSP must maintain its total independence and control.

The idea that some of the cost of the conflict resolution could be borne by the guilty state has also been suggested in this work. The exacting of reparations must be done very carefully. If one is not careful, and the reparations are too severe, the populace will suffer. They are often the innocents. The seeds of future hatred and conflict will, thereby, be sown. That does not mean, however, that reparations are not in order. What then should be the criteria for the establishment of the amount of the reparations?

If occupation is necessary the criteria for the amount of reparation must not exceed the direct cost to the UGSP and/or the UN for the conflict resolution and the occupation of the problem state. With that upper limit established, the reparation should be a percentage of the occupied state's GNP that will not impede the economic recovery and growth of the occupied state.

The major goal of occupying and administrating a state that has caused a world peace-threatening conflict is to return that state as a stable, productive state to the world community of states. A major contribution to its return to stability and prosperity will be the development of national resources. Those resources may be in the form of natural resources, agricultural resources, manufacturing ability and/or the intellectual abilities of the people. A percentage of the revenues derived from the development of the resources could be used to offset the cost to the UGSP and the UN. If the percentage which is used to offset cost is not punitive, local resentment should be minimized. In order to insure that the amount is not punitive, careful study of both the short term and long term economic effects must be made. The process will require constant vigilance, flexibility and "fine tuning". The development of the resources and the employment created will also assist in the "winning of the hearts and minds" of the people. In short, the development of the national resources can offset some of the cost and contribute to the possibility of national economic independence.

In closing this section it should be emphasized that if the UGSP is effective and there exists a greater degree of world stability, the need for extensive UGSP operations should decrease, and therefore its cost of maintenance should also decrease. It could be argued that, in the long run, it might cost less to maintain the UGSP than states currently spend on defense. Besides a more stable world, there would be a host of wealthier states.

CHAPTER ELEVEN

THE PEACEFUL SETTLEMENT OF DISPUTES

In the first of the Eight Principals which will guide UGSP actions outlined in Chapter Seven, there was a discussion of the criteria for the types of conflict in which the UGSP would have an interest. Now this work will address problems within a state or between two or more states that do not yet require UGSP intervention and/or ways to prevent the necessity of UGSP intervention.

As with many states of the world, the United States has a civil legal system in which two aggrieved parties can sue one another. Those lawsuits can be settled by arbitration or by a decision of a court. Depending on the type of case, compliance with the decision can be a problem. In some cases there is voluntary compliance. In other cases it becomes necessary for the court to force compliance through fines or criminal prosecution. Finally, through the ability to record liens, compliance is achieved by the lack of the ability of the losing party to conduct business with others until the lien, which is a judgment, has been satisfied. In both civil and criminal cases the courts can call upon the police powers of the state to enforce the court's edicts.

These principals of law should be applied on a worldwide scale. Indeed, there exists today some of the basic structure. What is lacking is consistency, the ability to enforce the compliance and the cooperation of states in the enforcement of a judgment.

The UN could be an excellent forum for the arbitration of international disputes. Unfortunately, the lack of consistency comes into play. Within the UN too many international disputes are dealt with in terms of politics and economic advantage instead of justice. Therefore, no one is satisfied, and the opinion or decision of the UN is either weak or ignored. Structurally, what the UN could and should do is develop a pool of states from across the international spectrum to be potential arbitrators. The parties to the dispute would then each appoint, as an example, two or three states to sit as arbitrators and the Security Council would then appoint one additional state as an additional arbitrator. These arbitrators could be called the "Council of Arbitration". Composed of the five to seven states, the Council of Arbitration would then hear the case and arrive at a binding resolution. This type of structure would go a long way toward removing political and economic influences and thereby render the decision based on justice. Typically, "binding resolution" means just that, there is no appeal or subsequent lawsuit. The formation of a UN Council of Arbitration would not replace the ICJ. Rather, the Council of Arbitration could serve the UN as a "scaled back" version of the ICJ. Properly administered, the Council of Arbitration could be a fast, efficient method of settling minor disputes and thus saving all parties extended grief. It could also free the ICJ for the consideration of more serious matters.

If the parties in dispute were to agree to binding arbitration, compliance with the decisions of the Council of Arbitration must be enforced. In the event of non-binding arbitration where there occurs the absence of voluntary compliance, the parties could be directed to appeal the case to the ICJ.

As with any appellate court, the ICJ could uphold the decision of the UN's Council of Arbitration, order it returned to the Council for further consideration, or invalidate the Council's decision. In that event, the ICJ must be specific and clear in the reasoning behind the invalidation, and it must make recommendations for the remedy. The ICJ could have the power to overrule the Council's decision and impose a different, enforceable judgment.

As for direct tools of enforcement available to the UN, the first, of course, is the imposition of sanctions. Sanctions have been utilized with varying degrees of success. Part of the problem has been the non-compliance by states other than the offending state with the terms of the sanctions. There are a variety of reasons for that lack of cooperation. In many cases, states have put their economic or political interest ahead of the sanctions. They may have done so because they believe the sanctions were unfairly imposed. In a more self-serving manner some states may ignore or violate the sanctions because they recognize the UN's lack of either the will or the ability to enforce the sanctions. By making the judgments based on justice rather than politics, some states will cooperate with the sanctions based on a belief of the fairness of the judgment. For those who still will not cooperate with the sanctions the UN should enact a resolution which states that a non-cooperating state risks the imposition of like sanctions upon themselves. If the UN were to develop a history of the uniform application of these principals it would cause an increasing number of voluntary compliances with the decisions of the proposed Council of Arbitration or the ICJ.

If it should become necessary, the UN could call upon the UGSP to enforce compliance with the decisions of the Council of Arbitration. The ICJ could call upon the UGSP to enforce compliance with ICJ decisions. In these cases the UGSP would, as outlined previously, conduct its own investigation as to whether or not it should intervene. Once again, if the UGSP has had a history of being consistent in executing its edicts, the order of the UGSP may cause a voluntary compliance.

Some aggrieved parties may wish to take their case directly to the ICJ for resolution. In the past, the ICJ has not had a definite, well defined enforcement vehicle. The UGSP would be that enforcement vehicle. There could be some cases that are presented to the ICJ where either the Court or the UGSP determines that it is a case for which they do not believe they should become involved. In that event, the ICJ, in declining to hear the case, would advise the parties to seek UN arbitration through the Council of Arbitration. The purpose of this provision is to prevent aggrieved parties from frivolous attempts to use the UGSP as their military force.

So far in this discussion this work has been primarily addressing disputes between states. What can be done about some disputes or oppressions that are strictly within a state? Several examples come quickly to mind. In some states, strictly within their national boundaries, there are "warlords" or tribes engaged in armed conflict and acts of terrorism in which innocent people are caught in the crossfire. In other cases, a regime has come to power that is so repressive as to cause widespread suffering to the population. These situations would draw the interest of the UGSP. Often these situations eventually cross national boundaries and thereby would become of interest to the UGSP. Now we would have issues of sovereignty. However, some situations are so severe, such as crimes against humanity against the offending state's own population that if the issue is given international scrutiny, national sovereignty may need to be discounted. Given the offending parties recognition of possible UGSP intervention, it could be possible to establish a peaceful solution through negotiations, mediation or litigation.

Within the above described national problems, who are the parties and how can they get their cases heard? Competing warlords or tribes and/or the national government, if one exists, could file suit in the same manner as states in dispute. In these cases the UN, the ICJ and the UGSP would follow the same course of action as discussed above. The same would be true for representatives of an oppressed people. This author recognizes that it may not be possible, given the degree of internal warfare or oppression, for aggrieved parties to file, much less prosecute, their suits. It may well be that an organization outside the state files and prosecutes a suit on behalf of a suffering population. There are a number of international humanitarian organizations that could fill that role. It could well be that a concerned state or states could also represent a party. Again, the UN, the ICJ and the UGSP would follow the course of action outlined above.

Currently, there are sometimes contradictory or confusing International Law criteria for the intervention in the internal affairs of states in which violations of human rights, genocide or crimes against humanity occur. The world has witnessed unnecessary killings while the UN has reacted slowly or not at all. As previously discussed, there are cases where the UGSP should not wait for the UN, the ICJ or the ICC to consider a case. In these cases, as rarely happens in today's world, common sense and humanity must trump politics. The UGSP should act swiftly.

There are, in the beginning of the twenty-first century, conflicts and disputes which cry out for arbitrated, enforceable settlements. If the UGSP were in existence and if the UGSP, the UN and the ICJ could function as this work has argued, some of those conflicts could be settled by enforceable arbitration. Some cases should be noted because they are so potentially dangerous: 1.) the Israeli/Palestinian conflict; 2.) the Indian/Pakistani dispute over Kashmir; and 3.) the China/Taiwan issue are cases in point.

With respect to the Israeli/Palestinian conflict there are some aspects which fall under the purview of this work. One of those aspects concerns objective arbitration as opposed to arbitration influenced by the political and/ or economic interest of the arbitrators. The United States has done a poor job as an arbitrator. Whatever the merits of the Israeli or the Palestinian cases may be, the Palestinians are correct in their position that the United States is biased in favor of Israel. The entire world is cognizant of the relationship between Israel and the United States. Both Israel and the United States consider each other as their "staunches" ally in Middle East affairs. Additionally, there exists within the United States a wealthy, politically powerful Jewish community. Through political campaign contributions and the ability to influence a large voting bloc, that community has a great deal of influence on the policies of the United States. That American politicians, congressmen and senators would allow such power influence and campaign contributions to influence their vote is shameful. This is not anti-Semitism on the part of this author. If the United States was biased toward the Palestinians and the Palestinians exerted financial influence over Congress, the criticism would be the same. Although not acknowledged in the Muslim world, the United States does provide the Palestinians with a considerable amount of aid.

If the UGSP, the UN and the ICJ could function as argued in this work, a just, enforceable settlement could be imposed on the Israelis and the Palestinians. Even though the United States would be a member state of the UGSP, it would have only one vote, or the United States could recuse itself, and would be duty bound to honor and help enforce the edicts of the UGSP. The realization of unbiased justice and the loss of a patron might open some new avenues of discussion for settlement between the parties. It is recognized that "healing the wounds" might take a long time, if ever.

India and Pakistan need help in their dispute. Since 1947, when they were separated into two states, through the year 2000 they have fought three wars. Yet, sadly, particularly in the Kashmir region, they are essentially the same people, even though the Pakistanis are primarily Muslim and the Indians are primarily Hindu. Families are divided by the borders and by the dispute. National pride, accusations of subversion and terror, and egos are hampering dialogue between these two states with nuclear capabilities. This is an extremely dangerous, world stability-threatening problem. It is possible their dispute could be resolved by the actions described above.

China could be a valuable member state within the UGSP. However, its dispute with Taiwan with respect to Taiwanese sovereignty must be resolved. Too many other states, including the United States, could become involved with disastrous consequences. Again, without going into the merits of the case, if China were a member of the UGSP, a peaceful settlement of that problem could be a condition of membership. As an alternative to that condition, China, if honorable, could recuse itself from any vote on a settlement if the UGSP were to become involved. In today's world, this author recognizes that this notion is fanciful.

The China/ Taiwan issue brings to the fore a rather interesting point. What if the offending party is a large powerful nation? How would the UGSP enforce either its edicts or the decisions of the UN, the ICJ or the ICC? Clearly an attempt by the UGSP to occupy a country such as Russia, China or the United States would spell international disaster. Here the threat or the imposition of potentially economically damaging trade sanctions would probably be the only course of action. In the world of the twenty-first century most developed or developing states realize that their interests are better served with a briefcase, not a missile. Given the state of development of the powerful states of the world, not one of them really wants a world war.

Here then is the key to this discussion. If there exists a UGSP which is consistent with the enforcement of its edicts, if it is swift and sure in its actions and the world has come to believe UGSP resolve, there will be more negotiated settlements of disputes. Additionally, if the UN, the ICJ and the ICC would offer just forums as outlined above, more states would be encouraged to utilize those arenas. Lastly, if the states of the world were to realize that the UN, the ICJ and the ICC are consistent and just and that, if necessary, their decisions would likely be enforced by the UGSP, there would be far more negotiating and far less warring.

CHAPTER TWELVE

GUNS OR BUTTER

There is an economic principal that holds that a state can produce guns or butter, but not both. That is not entirely true. However, its basic premise is sound. The term "guns" is used in this work to mean the production of military weapons for the expansion of power or influence and the maintenance of a standing military. It does not refer to the production of weapons for individual self-defense or sport shooting. The term "butter" refers to consumer goods and services. A state can produce both guns and butter, but not both at high levels for a sustained period of time. Additionally, as compared to butter, there is very little "value added" to the production of guns. The production of butter is a positive in a society and its economy. The production of guns for military purposes, is only for the destruction of something.

The above is not an argument for not producing any guns. As stated above, there are some legitimate uses such as defense of the state, self-defense, law enforcement and sport. Rather, it is an argument for the limitation of production so that economic resources can be better employed. It is also an argument for the limitation of the production of arms for world trade.

In his farewell speech in 1961, President of the United States Dwight D. Eisenhower warned against the influence of the "military-industrial complex". He argued that their size and power could have an undue influence on world policy. He was right. Around the world the production and sale of arms has become so enormous that it consumes a dangerously high percentage of economic output and industrial capacity in many states. On the one hand, too many states are spending unsustainable amounts of money to acquire weapons at the expense of vitally needed consumer goods. On the other hand, the economies of some states have become so dependent upon the production of arms that they do not believe they could slow production without causing grave economic damage. Certainly, the producers of those arms constantly promote that notion. Yet, nothing could be further from the truth. All state's resources are finite. The production of vast quantities of arms robs an economy of the ability to produce consumer goods. Granted, the reduction would cause adjustments, but those adjustments could be absorbed. If one does not believe that truth, one has only to look at the economy and the output of the United States immediately after World War Two. Warplane and tank factories became or returned to, auto, refrigerator and washing machine factories and they prospered. They prospered because there was a backlog of unsatisfied demands for consumer goods and services.

Around the world there is no shortage of the demand for consumer goods and services. If the industrialized states of the world would shift their focus from arms to consumer goods they would have the markets. This is particularly true if trade barriers were relaxed and manufacturing facilities were expanding in developing states thus providing employment. It is argued that the developed world cannot be competitive with the low labor costs of emerging states. Contrary to popular arguments, relaxed trade barriers would increase prosperity in the developing world. That enhanced prosperity should produce higher wages in those states. Additionally, that enhanced prosperity should increase the demand by them for commerce from the developed world.

If large quantities of weapons were not available, states would have more money to spend on consumer goods and services, and the incentives for the development of their productive economies. Hopefully, it would also reduce the availability of arms acquisition by terrorist groups. This is not a "pipe dream". However, this author recognizes that these proposals will be difficult to embrace. Enormous adjustments must be made, and they must be done gradually to prevent massive economic disruption. These proposals, however, are important goals which the states of the world must achieve.

If there existed a UGSP as outlined in this work, the higher degree of world security would decrease the need for states to believe they need to be heavily armed for defense. The UGSP would prevent rogue states from acquiring the weapons in the first place. To achieve that level of security and the limitations on potential rogue states, the world needs the UGSP and its enforcement capability. The states of the world must believe in that capability and the sureness of enforcement. Only then will those states be willing, probably grudgingly at first, to reduce their arms acquisition. By the same token, if the states which supply arms to the world would act more responsibly, the task of the UGSP would be far less difficult.

Wittingly, or unwittingly, the arms-producing states of the world promote conflict. They certainly facilitate conflict. Those governments must overrule their arms producing industries and limit the production and international sale of unwarranted quantities of arms. They must also limit the sale to irresponsible or belligerent states. Those governments must resist the financial assistance to their politicians by the arms industries. Those governments may want to provide incentives for the arms industries to decrease arms production and increase the production of consumer goods.

Who are the arms producing states that we are concerned with in this discussion? Some of them include, but are not limited to, the United States, Great Britain, France, Russia, China, Sweden and Germany. These are among the very countries that we have considered as member states of the UGSP. So how do we reconcile the dichotomy? By forming the UGSP these states and the other member states could consolidate, modernize and reduce their military. They could lead by example. For instance, they could and should destroy or vastly reduce their stockpiles of chemical, biological and nuclear weapons. If that does not encourage others to do the same, such as Iran and North Korea, the UGSP could legitimately order the destruction of those weapons. States could prevent the sale of nuclear potential material to states who are not nuclear powers. If necessary, the UGSP could prevent other states from becoming nuclear powers. States such as North Korea, who produce weapons as their major marketable industry for the express purpose of aiding rogue states, would be dealt with by the UGSP. States such as North Korea must be convinced to convert their industrial capability from weapons such as missiles to consumer goods. If they are unwilling to do so the UGSP would have an interest in that state's policies.

It bears repeating. The elimination of military arms production is not the issue. To be sure, there needs to be the production and the technological advancement of weapons. This is particularly true if the UGSP is to have the necessary capability to combat an ever changing, more sophisticated, terrorist oriented, rogue threat to world peace. Additionally, all states have the right to a defense capable of protecting the state and its citizens. The issue is about the irresponsible production and the proliferation of quantities of weapons.

If the UGSP could be successful in giving the world a greater sense of security, the states of the world could re-focus from arms to consumer goods and services. That increase in beneficial economic activity would create more prosperous states including the so called "third world" states. Prosperous or economically growing people are far less likely to be belligerent.

What has been argued here is not new. These ideas have been dreamed about and discussed for centuries. However, the results have never been achieved. Why? In this author's opinion it is because there has never been an effective means of enforcing peace. The UGSP is needed because man has never voluntarily insured peace.

CHAPTER THIRTEEN

OIL IS NOT FOREVER

In the beginning of the twenty-first century the West and parts of Asia are the greatest producers and consumers of goods and services in the world. They are so in numbers far greater than their proportionate share of the world's population. This will probably not change in the foreseeable future.

Technology is moving so fast that if a state's economy does not keep pace, that economy will likely be left behind and be far poorer as a result. Part of the technological advances will impact oil as an energy source. It is quite likely that before world reserves of oil are in jeopardy, oil will be replaced as a major energy source. Good examples are the rapid development of the fuel cell, wind power, solar power and the advancement of the electric automobile as efficient, cost effective, power generating systems.

Many of the oil producing states are in the Middle East. Many of the governments of those states are not sharing the oil wealth with their general population. Many of those states are not educating their people for future economic gain. For many of those states oil is the only, or at least the major, current economic asset. Much of the world security-threatening unrest is coming from the very same states who are not planning for a future without oil.

It does not take a great deal of intelligence to see the connection between the above facts. Nor does it take a great deal of intelligence to see what must be done. Yet it would appear that the states involved are doing precious little to avoid a future monumental disaster. That disaster may not be very far in the future. It would appear that several governments are looking only to their own personal enrichment with little concern for their general population or the future of their respective state. It may become necessary for the UGSP to plan actions that would put a halt to the world security unrest originating in this part of the world.

The states of the Middle East and Southwest Asia must establish and accomplish several goals concurrently:

1. They must recognize that unrest comes from deprivation. They must no longer allow the "Great Satan", the United States and its western allies, to be the excuse or scapegoat for religion-based terrorism. They must face the fact that the problems are within their own states. A satisfied and prosperous populace is rarely one that creates disorder.

2. They must rid their governments of rampant corruption.

3. While oil is still a valuable commodity, those governments must utilize some of that revenue for quality public services, infrastructure, healthcare and education. They must educate their population for future economic endeavors and begin to develop additional and alternative economic enterprises before the inevitable reduction in oil demand occurs.

4. They must recognize and thereby teach their citizens that the West and economically growing parts of Asia are not going to go away. They must educate their citizens to the fact that the West is not a threat to their national, cultural or religious sovereignty. They must recognize and educate their citizens that the West and Asia are an economic and technologic force to be joined for their own well-being and future prosperity. In short, the Middle East and Southwest Asia and its people must make actual, ideological and philosophical peace with the rest of the world. To not do so would be a grave social mistake.

5. They must recognize that their well-being and security is impacted by the health of their neighboring states. Just as the West, led by the United States, spends a great deal on foreign aid, so too must the oil rich states of the Middle East invest in the future prosperity of the non-oil producing states of the Middle East, Southwest Asia and help with aid to Africa.

If these states will make the above efforts in a manner that is clearly recognized by their citizens, they should be winning the support of their population. Concurrently, they must take the steps necessary to eliminate the terrorist cells and groups within their respective states which threaten both their state's and the world's security.

The reality is that if these states do not take the above steps they risk chaos and revolution from their own citizens. The world is witnessing examples of this internal unrest within several of these states. There is spillover into neighboring states. This unrest, rebellion and subsequent terrorism will heighten at the point when oil is no longer in high demand and the population of those states become even more impoverished.

In summary, if these states do not recognize that oil is not forever and fail to take the above steps, they will be greatly reduced in economic influence. They will enjoy little diplomatic power because they will have little to offer. They will find themselves overpowered if they become a world security threat. Today, some of these events are already occurring.

If the leaders of many of these states are unable or unwilling to take the above steps, the UGSP could execute actions in this part of the world to insure world security.

CHAPTER FOURTEEN

THE WAR ON DRUGS

So far this work has been addressing the control, or rather the elimination, of potential or actual violent threats to world security. There exists, however, another major threat to world stability. That threat is the worldwide epidemic of illegal drugs and the resultant crime, gang warfare, violent drug cartels, state unrest and addictions. It is a major threat to the social order within most states whether they are the suppliers of illegal drugs, the consumers of illegal drugs, or both. Additionally, the illegal drug trade is a major source of revenue for the procurement of weapons by terrorist organizations.

Using the United States as an example, illegal drugs are responsible for a disproportionately high percentage of crime. These crimes include, but are not limited to: murder; violent injury; gang warfare; robbery; smuggling; fraud and conspiracy. This is the business side of illegal drugs and the illegal profits are enormous. In nation/states that are the suppliers of illegal drugs, turf wars and power struggles erupt into bloody confrontations in which innocent people are killed or wounded and governments are destabilized.

The use of illegal drugs is also responsible for criminal and accidental injury, death, and property damage while under the influence of illegal drugs. Illegal drugs are responsible for a great deal of mental and physical illness, social unrest and family breakdowns. Illegal drugs cause great financial drains and place strains on local, state and federal resources. These are resources that could be used for the social good. The United States has been used here as the example. However, the same problems occur in many other states around the world.

Those who would advocate making illegal drugs legal and thereby controlling the manufacture and distribution are, at best, naive. From the outset, the drug lords would do everything in their rather considerable power to prevent legalization. While legalization might reduce some crime, it does nothing to reduce the health and social problems of drug addiction.

Those who would advocate focusing on curing addiction and thereby eliminating the demand are equally naive. It has been tried and, indeed, is an ongoing effort. It has not been successful. Some people argue that the effort to eliminate the supply and imprison the suppliers and dealers has also not been successful. In that observation they are right. The cause for the failure to eliminate the supply and the suppliers of illegal drugs is the result of not bringing the available resources to bear against this worldwide threat.

Because the illegal drug traffic is international in scope and is thereby a global security threat, it would be an area of legitimate interest to the UGSP. In fact, all too often, drug trafficking is a violent threat to world security. The UGSP could and should employ the exact same tactics that would be employed in eliminating any other violent threat to world security. The UGSP could assume the lead, thereby relieving individual states, in the elimination of the worldwide trafficking of illegal drugs. This would vastly increase the resources, power, authority and efficiency in the winning the war on drugs.

As with other violent threats, the UGSP should bring its combined intelligence gathering capabilities to bear. Through the use of that intelligence the UGSP would know exactly who are the problem individuals and groups, both within and without a government, and their exact locations, movements and methods of operation. The UGSP would then formulate the plan of action that follows the same criteria as in any other violent conflict. The UGSP, recognizing that many government officials profit from illegal drugs because corruption is rife, would have no tolerance for the illegal drug trade.

It would seem that intervention by the UGSP in the manufacture and distribution of illegal drugs would be an affront to a state's sovereignty. Part of that problem comes about because the drug trade is, in many cases, not as visible as other violent threats. As with most forms of terrorism, the drug threat and violence hides in the shadows. It is quite elusive. However, by its very nature and scope, it is a world problem which routinely crosses borders. The drug cartels have the power to bring down governments.

With the assistance of the UGSP, the fact is that many states such as the United States could redeploy much of their drug fighting resources internally rather than having to fight the problem internationally on their own.

CHAPTER FIFTEEN

SUMMARY AND FINAL THOUGHTS

I t is important to put forth the idea of the UGSP at a time when there are great world security-threatening situations. There is no question but what it is a concept that requires a great deal of vision, planning and cooperation between states dedicated to world peace. If it is even possible to form a UGSP there are challenges which must be faced in attracting member states. There are great obstacles which must be overcome with respect to national sovereignty concerns.

This final section will deal with other issues that will require inquiry and study. In fact this entire work is intended to be an overview. The subjects below, as with most of the subjects and ideas presented throughout this work, should be the objects of much greater study.

Checks and Balances

When instituting an organization or government it is reassuring to know that there are checks on the decisions and actions of that organization or government. That is, the organization or government cannot initiate actions that are not subject to review. If necessary, such checks could modify the proposed action or rescind it entirely. For example, that is the principle behind the formation of the government of the United States. There are three branches of the United States government, the Executive, the Legislative and the Judiciary. They are designed to initiate policy and law, and they are designed to review each other's decisions. With the UGSP "checks and balances" will only occur with the internal debate and the vote of the member states.

The UN, the ICJ, the ICC, or individual states might object to or have problems with certain plans of action of the UGSP. The fact is, there would be no individual power with the ability to prevent the UGSP from following a particular course of action. As we have formulated the criteria for the establishment of the UGSP, the most militarily and economically powerful states would be the states that make up the UGSP. This fear of an all-powerful organization with its armed force capability and its ability to negate state sovereignty are the greatest arguments against the formation of the UGSP. This may well be the reason one has never been formed.

How then, does one control the actions of the UGSP? As a practical matter, no one would be able to do so. However, the UGSP would be created from a cross section of states, geographical and ideological. There would be a process of investigation that includes excellent intelligence, input, advice and the testimony of all interested parties, organizations and governments. Because of the diversity of the states that make up the UGSP and the presumed intelligence of the representatives of those states, fair decisions should be achieved. Indeed, for the UGSP to be effective, their decisions must be final. There must be no question as to outcome.

While it is an unlikely event, should a member state of the UGSP be in gross violation of the principles of the UGSP, a mechanism for expelling that member should be in place. What is meant by "gross violation"? While not limited to the following, gross violations would include the desire of a member state to expand their territory at the expense of a neighboring state. Gross violations would also include supporting aggression or terrorism in a region for their own economic or political gain. Additionally, a "grievance committee" of member states should be established to hear the complaints of outside organizations or states as to the conduct of individual member states or the UGSP as a whole. Those grievances should be publicly aired and the results of the ultimate investigation and plan of action, if any, publicly announced. Admittedly, this is less than total reassurance to the rest of the world. However, the establishment of such mechanisms within the UGSP would demonstrate the good faith of the UGSP.

It is possible to have a powerful, yet altruistic, organization. In the beginning of the twenty-first century the United States is a good example. If, for example, the United States decided to annex Mexico, forcibly if necessary, who would be able to prevent it? There would be an enormous outcry to be sure, but who would want to risk the military consequence of attempting to stop the United States? The answer is that it is not even an issue. The United States has no desire to do so and it recognizes that that would not be an acceptable course of action in the world community of states. The answer is that, with respect to the UGSP, the same realizations would hold true. The answer is that peace, security and economic prosperity is the greatest priority to the states which are candidate members of the UGSP. Peace, security and prosperity must overshadow any aggressive motivations of the candidate states of the UGSP. The interest of the candidate states for world peace and security and the world's need for peace and security exactly mirror the goals and policies of the UGSP.

Sovereignty

If this were a perfect world the idea of a UGSP would not be necessary. We do not live in a perfect world. We never have and we never will. As was stated in the beginning of this work, since the dawn of man, mankind has been dreaming up more and more sophisticated methods of killing, maiming, torturing and dominating his fellow man. Therefore, if mankind is to survive, some powerful institutions and some well-planned compromises must be made to insure that survival and peace.

On a local and national level, societies live fairly successfully and peacefully with rules of law. The same basic concepts must be, and could be, expanded on an international scale. Unfortunately, while most states would agree with the basic goals, very few will allow those concepts to be applied to themselves. Most states take the position that no other state or group of states is going to exercise any kind of control over that state's "internal" affairs. Moreover, with rare exception, no state or group of states is likely to agree to allow their politicians, military commanders or individual soldiers to be put on trial. States fear that prosecutions could be politically motivated. If this sovereignty obstacle cannot be overcome there is not a prayer for the success of the UN "peacekeeping", the ICJ or the ICC. Admittedly, the ICC has had a few successful prosecutions. However, they have been rare. States simply will not comply unless it is convenient to do so.

How then does the world overcome the sovereignty issue? The issue of sovereignty is probably the largest single stumbling block to the formation of the UGSP.

The reality is that very few states will willingly agree to subordinate their sovereignty to any organization. The only probable way to deal with the issue is to convince potential member states of the UGSP that achieving world peace and security supersedes the sanctity of sovereignty. Unfortunately, and this appears arbitrary, given the criteria for enforced peacekeeping, sovereignty may have to be negated.

Tribes, towns, villages, cities, states, provinces and nation/states have a body of written law for the control of conduct. Many of those "bodies of written law" were written, and are reviewed and revised, by representatives elected by the governed. Most of those laws are understood by the governed as are the consequences of violation. Most of the resultant systems of justice and enforcement have safeguards to prevent unjust prosecution. The same could be done on an international scale.

Over the centuries, the states of the world have formed International Law. International Law comes in two forms. "Codified International Law" is a body of written statutes. "Customary International Law" is not written as such. Rather, it is established by precedence. There have been some good works. Unfortunately there is such a huge volume of "law" with only voluntary compliance for the most part. With such a large volume, some International Law is contradictory and open to wide interpretation. Therefore, there is no truly organized, concise body of International Law. The statesmen of the world have enough history, precedence, knowledge of human decency and common sense to draft a body of International Law which can be clearly understood for the enforcement of world security. The statesmen of this world must draft clearly defined *Primary Law* with clearly defined *Secondary Laws* for the enforcement of the Primary Laws. These International Laws can be drafted to clearly define what exactly constitutes a "war crime", a "crime against humanity" or what actions constitute a threat to world security. These International Laws can be drafted to safeguard individual people and states from unwarranted, frivolous or political prosecutions. The writing of these laws will require a great deal of careful planning and intelligence. It will require compromises on the part of states. However, it can be done if there is the will.

Dissention Is Not Always Terrorism

Very vocal opposition to a regime is not necessarily terrorism or a world threat. Indeed, many states, mainly in the West, jealously guard the right of free speech, free assembly and a free press. Armed conflict within a state is not necessarily terrorism or a world threat. If an individual or a group gives speeches, prints articles, holds rallies and demonstrations decrying the wrongs of a regime, that is dissention and it may very well be legitimate. That protest may even develop into armed revolution. It is in fact the very right of a citizenry to rise up in armed revolt against their government if that government is repressive and unresponsive to the legitimate grievances of the populace.

However, there is a point where a line has been crossed. If that same individual or group is advocating harm to the people of other states or the institutions of other states, the line has been crossed into terrorism and/or a world threat. If, for example, that individual or group is calling for like-minded individuals or groups to harm the people of a state wherever in the world they may be, that is terrorism and a world threat. If they are calling for the sabotage and destruction of another state's assets, that is terrorism and a world threat. If they are attempting in their cause to recruit combatants from other states that may very well be a world threat.

The Sharing Of Intelligence

As of the beginning of the twenty-first century, we are seeing that conflict and wars are rarely being fought by large armies on a battlefield. They are taking on the character of small groups employing guerrilla and/or terrorist tactics. They are tactics that are very difficult to defend against and no state is safe or immune. Therefore, it would not matter whether or not a state is a member state of the UGSP, it would be in everyone's security interest to cooperate with and contribute to the intelligence gathering capabilities of the UGSP.

The UGSP must establish an intelligence data base. That data base must include all the relevant information on the activities of potentially threatening individuals or groups. Anyone either questioned or arrested as a threat to a means of transportation or communication, worldwide, should have their information supplied to the data bank by the relevant agency or government. Anyone questioned or arrested for international drug trafficking or money laundering should be in the data bank. Any questionable international financial exchange should be in the data bank. Anyone questioned or arrested for the illegal possession of arms and/or threatening propaganda should likewise be in the data bank. However slight, anyone who has participated in a violent political act must be in the data base. While this list is not complete, the point is that, to affectively prevent disastrous events from occurring, vast amounts of information must be available. It must be possible to predict trends and identify connections that could lead to the apprehension of terrorists before they are able to act. It is recognized that there are some groups, watchdogs for individual liberties, rights and privacy that will argue against such measures. Sadly, the world has come to the point where some of those issues must be put aside. It would be hoped, however, that the UGSP would exercise sensitivity and prudence in these matters.

If there was worldwide cooperation in supplying data to the UGSP's intelligence data base, the UGSP would constantly monitor that data base. This is a daunting task with less than total success possible. Nonetheless, as a result of that monitoring the UGSP would be able to warn target states of a potential problem either within their borders or from abroad. If applicable, the UGSP might offer assistance. This course of action would lead to further cooperation and might prevent world threatening disasters.

No One State

This work has stated repeatedly that no one state can be the world's policeman by themselves. Throughout history it has been the downfall of great states and empires. It has been the downfall of those who attempted to control portions of the world greater than they could economically sustain on a long term basis.

In the beginning of the twenty-first century, this is the path that the United States is in great danger of following. It is a lesson of history that is being ignored by the United States. It is possible that the United States, in the first decades of the twenty-first century, does not believe it is yet a potential problem. It is.

Along with most states of the world, the United States spends more on its military than is probably necessary. The United States spends too much valuable time and money building temporary coalitions to stop a threat. It is very inefficient. Instead, a permanent world police force, the UGSP, would share the expense, be more militarily efficient and timely in stopping world security threatening problems and preventing others from even starting. With a United Global Security Partnership no one state would risk its long-term stability in an attempt to resolve world threatening conflicts. The burden would be shared.

Final Thoughts

At the very outset, this work established that the very idea of a UGSP would not be a popular notion. This work cited the sovereignty issues and the understandable fear of so powerful an organization. However, as this is written, many of the principles of a UGSP are being employed. Coalitions are formed, on a case by case basis, to put down a world destabilizing problem. There exists an ICJ and an ICC but they have very little ability to enforce their decisions. The UN, while an important world asset, is not as effective as it could be. The problem is that, while the principles are being employed, there is no consistency, no sure and unmistakable results. There is no credible, permanent, sure, deterrent to the rogues of this world.

It is an undeniable historical fact that man has not had the discipline to achieve lasting world peace and security. With the rapidly expanding technological advancements and the ability for small groups to do grievous damage, this lack of man's discipline is far more dangerous than at any time in the history of the world. Indeed, the very existence of civilization could be threatened. Given these facts, there is probably no other solution to world security other than making permanent the principles of the temporary coalitions. The world must have a permanent police force, the United Global Security Partnership.

REFERENCES

<u>Preface</u>

1. Locke, John, *Two Treatises On Government*, The author relied upon his memory of the 1962 undergraduate reading of John Locke. The publishing data is lost to the author.

2. In the first edition, no specific research was done in the writing of the book. The author relied primarily on over a half century interest in international affairs.

<u>Summary of the Plan</u>

1. Charter of the North Atlantic Treaty Organization, www.nato.int/docu/basictxt/treaty.htm

2. Charter of the Southeast Treaty Organization, www.bartleby.com/65/stEATO.html

Chapter 1

1. Kennedy, Paul, *The Rise And Fall of the Great Powers*, New York, Random House, 1987

Chapter 2

1. United Nations Office for Disarmament Affairs

Chapter 3

1. MacRae, Peter, *Twenty-First Century Violent Conflict: The Insufficiency of International Law*, San Diego, Montezuma Press, 2005

2. Ibid

3. Rome Statute Of The International Criminal Court, www.un.org/law/icc/statute

4. Charter of the North Atlantic Treaty Organization, www.nato.int/docu/basictxt/treaty.htm

5. Charter of the Southeast Treaty Organization, www.bartleby.com/65/stEATO.html

6. Kennedy, Paul, *The Rise And Fall of the Great Powers*, New York, Random House, 1987

Chapter 4

1. Portions of this chapter are excerpts from a graduate seminar paper by Peter MacRae in International Law, November, 2003

2. Charter of the United Nations, San Francisco: 1945, accessed Oct. 25, 2003; available From http://www.un.org/aboutun/charter/htm

3. Cassese, Antonio, International Law, Oxford: Oxford University Press, 2001, P.280

4. United Nations Charter, Chapter V

5. United Nations Charter, Chapter V

6. Nixon, Richard M., *Seize the Moment*, New York, Simon & Schuster, 1992, P.34. This grim statistic is well known. Nixon's citation is among many available.

7. United Nations Charter, Chapter V

8. Barker, J. Craig, International Law and International Relations, London: Continuum, 2000

9. Charter of the North Atlantic Treaty Organization, www.nato.int/docu/basictxt/treaty.htm

10. Charter of the Southeast Treaty Organization, www.bartleby.com/65/stEATO.html

Chapter 5

1. MacRae, Peter, *Twenty-first Century Violent Conflict: The Insufficiency of International Law*, San Diego, Montezuma Press, 2005. This chapter includes major excerpts from the author's Master's Degree Thesis.

2. Waltz, Kenneth, 1986, "Political Structures", in Robert Keohane (ed.), *Neorealism and Its Critics*, New York, Columbia University Press

3. The Charter of the United Nations

4. Bull, Hedley, *The Anarchical Society*, New York, Columbia University Press, 1995

5. Ibid

6. Vattel, E, de. 1758, "Introduction", *The Law of Nations*, Translated by the Carnegie Institute, 1916. Hedly Bull, *The Anarchical Society*, New York, Columbia University Press, 1995

7. Cassese, Antonio, *International Law*, Oxford, Oxford University Press, 2001

8. Falk, Richard, *Human Rights Horizons: The Pursuit of Justice in a Global World*, York, Routledge, 2000

9. Cassese, Antonio, *International Law*, Oxford, Oxford University Press, 2001

10. The Charter of the United Nations

11. Wright, Quincy, "The Concept of Aggression in International Law", *American Journal of International Law 29*, 1935

12. Lahnerman, William J., "Introduction", in William J. Lahnerman (ed.), *Military Intervention; Cases in Context for the Twenty-First Century*, Lanham, MD, Rowman & Littlefield, 2004

13. Falk, Richard, *Human Rights Horizons: The Pursuit of Justice in a Global World*, York, Routledge, 2000

14. Glennon, Michael J., *Limits of Law, Prerogatives of Power*, New York, Palgrave, 2001

15. Steinbruner, John, and Jason Forrester, "Perspectives on Civil Violence: A Review of Current Thinking", in William Laherman (ed.), *Military Intervention: Cases in Context for the Twenty-First Century*, Lanham, MD, Rowman & Littlefield, 2004. It is interesting to note that Steinbruner and Forrester refer to 156 major conflicts whereas Richard Nixon refers to 170. This discrepancy points out the difficulty of defining the nature of international conflict.

16. Nixon, Richard M., *Seize the Moment*, New York, Simon & Schuster, 1992, P.34.

17.	Steinbruner, John, and Jason Forrester, "Perspectives on Civil Violence: A Review of Current Thinking", in William Laherman (ed.), *Military Intervention: Cases in Context for the Twenty-First Century*, Lanham, MD, Rowman & Littlefield, 2004.

18.	Glennon, Michael J., *Limits of Law, Prerogatives of Power*, New York, Palgrave, 2001

19.	Ibid

20.	Byers, Michael and Simon Chesterman, "Changing Rules About Rules? Unilateral Humanitarian Intervention and the Future of International Law", in J.L. Holzgrefe and Robert Keohane (ed.), *Humanitarian Intervention: Ethics. Legal and Political Dilemmas*, Cambridge, Cambridge University Press, 2003

21.	Stromseth, Jane, "Rethinking Humanitarian Intervention: The Case for Incremental Change", in J. L. Holzgrefe and Robert O. Keohane (eds.), *Humanitarian Intervention*, Cambridge, Cambridge University Press, 2003

22.	Shultz, Richard H. and Vogt, Andreas, "The Real Intelligence Failure of 9/11 and the Case for a Doctrine of Striking First", in Russell Howard and Reid Sawyer (eds.), *Terrorism and Counterterrorism: Understanding the New Security Environment*, Guilford, CT., McGraw-Hill/Dushkin, 2004

23.	Cassese, Antonio, *International Law*, Oxford, Oxford University Press, 2001

Chapter 6

1.	International Court of Justice www.icj-cij.org

2.	Rome Statute Of The International Criminal Court, www.un.org/law/icc/statute 99_corr/cstatute.htm

3.	Bennett, Gordon, "The SVR Russia's Intelligence Service", The Conflict Studies Research Centre, Royal Military Academy Sandhurst, Surrey England, 2000

4. African Union Commission, Peace and Security Council,
   www.au.int/en/commision

Chapter 7

1. Blanchard, Christopher M., "Afghanistan: Narcotics and U. S. Policy",
   Congressional Research Service, October 7, 2009
2. CNN, "Hopes and Fears Over Trillion Dollar Minerals", Afghan
   Crossroads, August 25, 2010
3. Ibid
4. Ibid

Chapter 8

1. "Creation of Israel 1948", United States Department of State, Office
   of the Historian, Internet,
   history.state.gov/milestones/1945-1952/creation-israel

Chapter 10

1. Kennedy, Paul, *The Rise And Fall of the Great Powers*, New York,
   Random House, 1987

ABOUT THE AUTHOR

Peter MacRae holds a Master's Degree in International Relations from San Diego State University. His academic specialty deals with the inability of International Law to deal with twenty-first century violent conflict. During the Master's program he was the teaching assistant for upper division courses in International Conflict Resolution. As a result, his academic interest and studies expanded to include today's terrorism and terrorist organizations.

Mr. MacRae has written numerous unpublished essays on International Conflict, International Law and terrorism. He has three published works; the self-published *A Measured Response: The United Global Security Partnership (First Edition)*, *The Poppies of Mohammed*, a fact-based novel, and his Master's Thesis, *Twenty-first Century Violent Conflict: The Insufficiency of International Law*, published by Montezuma Press.

Besides his interest in world affairs, Mr. MacRae's recreational interests include fishing, spearfishing, boating, hiking, travel and cooking. As a former lifeguard for the City of San Diego, Mr. MacRae has been active in the

United States Lifesaving Association and the World Lifesaving Federation ocean rescue competitions.

Along with his wife Patricia, Mr. MacRae lives in the Wine Country of Northern California.

www.ingramcontent.com/pod-product-compliance
Lightning Source LLC
Chambersburg PA
CBHW072247310526
45795CB00011B/282